Mercedes-Benz
SUPERCARS
From 1901 to Today

Schiffer Publishing Ltd

4880 Lower Valley Road Atglen, Pennsylvania 19310

Other Schiffer Books on Related Subjects:

Alfa Romeo: A Century of Innovation, 978-0-7643-4072-7, $29.99

Harley-Davidson Legends, 978-0-7643-4073-4, $29.99

New York City Horsepower: An Oral History of Fast Custom Machines, 978-0-7643-3961-5, $50.00

Originally published as Mercedes-Benz Supersportswagen von 1901 bis heute by Heel Verlag GmbH
Photos and information on them:
Mercedes-Benz Archives & Collection, Dieter Rebmann
Design and layout:
Gb-s Mediendesign, Koenigswinter, Germany
Translated from the German by Dr. Edward Force

Library of Congress Control Number: 2012930369

Covers designed by: Bruce Waters
Type set in Gill Sans

ISBN: 978-0-7643-4090-1
Printed in China

Schiffer Books are available at special discounts for bulk purchases for sales promotions or premiums. Special editions, including personalized covers, corporate imprints, and excerpts can be created in large quantities for special needs. For more information contact the publisher:
Published by Schiffer Publishing Ltd.
4880 Lower Valley Road
Atglen, PA 19310
Phone: (610) 593-1777; Fax: (610) 593-2002
E-mail: Info@schifferbooks.com
For the largest selection of fine reference books on this and related subjects, please visit our website at
www.schifferbooks.com
We are always looking for people to write books on new and related subjects. If you have an idea for a book, please contact us at
proposals@schifferbooks.com
This book may be purchased from the publisher.
Include $5.00 for shipping.
Please try your bookstore first.
You may write for a free catalog.
In Europe, Schiffer books are distributed by
Bushwood Books
6 Marksbury Ave.
Kew Gardens
Surrey TW9 4JF England
Phone: 44 (0) 20 8392 8585; Fax: 44 (0) 20 8392 9876
E-mail: info@bushwoodbooks.co.uk
Website: www.bushwoodbooks.co.uk

Thomas Wirth

Mercedes-Benz
SUPERCARS
From 1901 to Today

Foreword

What exactly is a supercar?

The answer is, so it seems, not at all difficult. A supercar is a sure head-turner because it shows at once that it is faster, more expensive, more desirable than that which we simply call a sports car. So it is a sports car that can do everything a good bit better than one expects and hopes for. That is the simple idea that stands behind a supercar.

In the world of supercars, several laws apply. The usual yardsticks are just laughed at. It has always been like that: Every era builds its own supercars that stand out with their performance figures and handling, achievements that seemed unthinkable just a generation ago. And it is clear that it did not happen by chance, but results from a lot of thinking, a lot of constructive work, calculated courage—and not least, entrepreneurial risks.

Behind extreme automobiles there is always a small number of men and women who invest a little of their hearts' blood in their projects. In all professionalism, in

all physical values, and despite a limited budget, they also dream this dream. In fact, more intensively than those who drive it later. Without these dreams there would be no supercars.

Supercars began very early. They are by no means an invention of the 1980s, as some people like to claim. The first representatives of this exclusive class were not the Ferrari F40 and the Porsche 959. Supercars began earlier, much earlier. At that time Mercedes surprised the world with a model that was simply called "35 HP" and did nothing less than stand the automotive world on its head.

The new concept was radical: The car was stronger and lighter, and thus much faster. And much safer, because its new frame provided a wider track and a much lower center of gravity. That was not a lucky chance, but rather the result of hard work—and the steadfast wish of (as we would say today) a racing-stable owner and marketing genius.

Supercars form the automotive spearheads of their eras. In the early days of the automobile and motorsports, they were still identical to the racing car. What competed for trophies on the road on Sunday spent the weekdays on the streets of town. But in 1903 the ways of the two genres began to separate. Racing cars followed the growing number of specific definitions for motorsport, while the supercars among the production vehicles offered their prosperous customers all the fun of driving what was legally usable on the street.

Such enthusiasm arises from many facets. The design is of great importance, but technology is no less so, uniting the most modern and best possibilities of the time. And naturally, the performance data has to make sense. From these engineering masterpieces that everyone knew, and only a few could afford, the dreams of many always arose.

As different as Mercedes-Benz supercars have naturally been over almost 110 years, they are all fascinating. They are exciting. And they are all desirable, each one in its very own way. They blend smoothly into a series, although their characters are very varied, as this book shows. Every era characterizes the cars that arise in it. They mirror their era, and they do it especially when they are such sources of emotional joy.

No other marquee can build on such a long tradition in supercars. Mercedes-Benz has presented a supercar in a unique manner to the present day. The wealth of models is striking in such an exquisite class. This book attempts, for the first time, to draw the great line from the 35 HP Mercedes introduced in 1901 to the present-day SLS AMG. These cars seem to be a universe apart. But something essential unites them: ingenious authenticity—and stunning fascination.

Enjoy the Mercedes-Benz supercars!

Contents

The Great Race Begins

With the first Mercedes, the Daimler Motoren Gesellschaft invents the supercar in 1901. This radical new design has nothing more to do with the high-bodied motor coaches. It points the young automobile's way to a successful future.

There it is indeed, that day when the first Mercedes supercar rolled onto the street—on November 22, 1900, the brand new car had to show, on a trip to Ludwigsburg, what it could do. And that was a whole lot. More than the designers had expected: The luxuriant 35 HP tear at the chassis of the car so wildly that they decide to strengthen the chassis considerably.

In the autumn of 1900 this car amounts to a little miracle—less for its technical equipment, to be sure, more for the company distancing the car from motorsport. The leadership of the Cannstatt Daimler-Motoren-Gesellscheft looks somewhat critically upon that. It is no wonder, for just half a year earlier there had been a serious auto accident. On March 30, 1900, Wilhelm Bauer had taken part in the Nice-La Turbie mountain climb with a Daimler Phoenix racing car. The road had been wet, and spectators are said to have run around on the course, which caused Wilhelm Bauer to slow down on the first curve. He lost control of the high, bucking car, struck the stone wall and was badly injured. On the next day he succumbed to his injuries.

This news hit one man hard. Emil Jellinek was crushed. It was he who had hired Wilhelm Bauer as the driver of his Phoenix—posing as a racing-stable owner. A successful businessman, Jellinek was born in Leipzig and was a sportsman and an artist of life who had been around. He was completely enthralled by speed. He was one of those gentlemen drivers who enthusiastically took part regularly in the Nice Racing Week. He entered there, as usual in those social circles, under a pseudonym. He called his team "Mercedes," the name of his ten-year-old daughter—who, by the way, never in her life showed any interest in automobiles.

"Monsieur Mercedes," as Emil Jellinek called himself, drove Daimler-Motoren-Gesellschaft since 1897. For him it was no longer just a toy, but also a coolly calculated business. In the mild south of France there were enough financially strong and sufficiently bored people who enjoyed that luxury article, the automobile. Motorsport, for

dealer Jellinek, had long been one thing above all else: the best advertising for his products. "Racing makes the name of a factory and a marquee," Jellinek said.

For that very reason, Jellinek did not think of giving up. Quite the opposite, and now, three days after the tragic accident in Nice, he signed a contract with representatives of the Daimler-Motoren-Gesellschaft that assured him far-reaching sales rights. And more: He worked out that a new generation of Daimler cars in the future should bear the name "Mercedes." A little later, Jellinek even commented: "An auto must bear a woman's name, to be fond of and pamper." At this time Jellinek already ranked among the most important customers of the Daimler-Motoren-Gesellschaft, and was at once their best PR and marketing expert. They listened to his wishes and requirements.

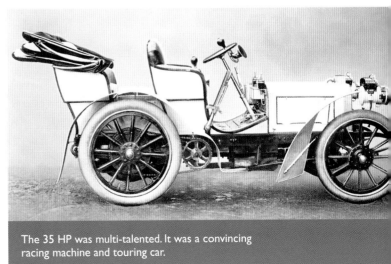

The 35 HP was multi-talented. It was a convincing racing machine and touring car.

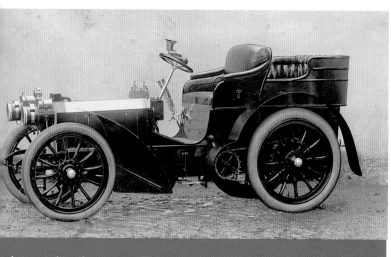

A practical gentleman racer: The rear, with the second seat, can be unscrewed.

And they come not long after Wilhelm Bauer's tragic accident. A completely new design must be created by Daimler Chief Designer Wilhelm Maybach, says Jellinek. Safer and easier to handle, the new car must be, no longer so long-legged, but absolutely stronger and faster. Thus he spoke—and gave an order for 36 examples of various Daimler cars at a value of 550,000 gold Marks. Just a little later, a second order followed. Jellinek gave the impulses, which fired up the inspired technician Wilhelm Maybach. Maybach himself did not dream of racing, but developing a suitable automobile for it was a task that motivated him highly. Nothing moved him more than thinking and rethinking out technology radically. He and his colleagues needed only about half a year until the new 35-hp car was running. The displacement had now grown to almost six liters (360 cu in), the inlet valves were controlled by a second camshaft, there were two carburetors, whose technology Maybach had clearly refined. But the most outstanding innovation concerned the cooling system, which had often caused big trouble until then: Maybach's new honeycomb radiator, so called because of the square shape of his 8,070 short tubes, is many times more effective than the former solution. Only this new cooling system made the clear increase in performance possible.

It had a frame of pressed steel, likewise an innovation. It had a clearly longer wheelbase and a wider track. Now the engine can be mounted deeper in the frame; thus the new car weighs 1,000 kg (~2,200 lbs), almost a third lighter. Newfound technologies like a crankcase of thin-walled cast aluminum save a lot of weight.

All of that impressed Jellinek's mechanic Hermann Braun, who took the new product out on a four-hour test run in Cannstatt on December 15, 1900. He was excited—the first Mercedes drove phenomenally. The engine ran uncommonly quietly, had a stable idle, and accelerated unbelievably strongly. Such a thing had never existed before.

A great gamble had succeeded for Wilhelm Maybach. He had not only improved countless details, but essentially reworked the automobile, fourteen years after its invention, as a total creation. Nothing was reminiscent of that high-bodied block of a Daimler Phoenix any more, yet it had been timely until a short time earlier. The suggestion of a coach from which one had stolen the wagon-tongue is now finally passé. From now on the driver sat in and no longer on the car. The new layout looked flat and extended, incredibly modern. The 35-hp car was exactly what Jellinek had desired in his order: "Light, fast, and beautiful," had been his words. Emil Jellinek was not only excited about Wilhelm Maybach's technical virtuosity, but also by his speed in realizing his ideas: "He can invent on command," trade expert Jellinek exults.

Further data of this first supercar, also the first Mercedes of all time, are known. For example, the first specimen was sent on its way from Cannstatt on December 22, 1900, to Nice, where in March 1901 the Mercedes 35 HP will take part in the racing weeks. Baron Henri de Rothschild, whose pseudonym is Dr. Pascal, sends Wilhelm Werner. Later chauffeur of the German Kaiser, Daimler works Werner into the race. With great success, Werner and his Mercedes 35 HP wins almost everything that can be won: the prestigious La Turbie mountain climb, the sprint as well as the long-run evaluation, the latter covering over 392 kilometers. At some places the car reaches 90 kph (~56 mph).

Sportier than all the others: the 35 HP with its convincingly low center of gravity.

The competitors have no chance against the triumphantly performing new Mercedes. The French press openly comments in the *Auto Velo* journal: "One must admit after this achievement that in Germany, not only the building of engines, nothing else being expected from the Daimler works, but also in automobile building, great progress has been made." Openly and somewhat depressed, Paul Meyan, the Secretary-General of the Automobile Club of France, adds up the score after the racing week: "We have entered the Mercedes era."

After this smashing success in racing, the Mercedes 35 HP, promptly fitted with a four-seat touring-car body, excites the elegant world sauntering along the boulevards of Nice. In this form it seems more civil, and its weight is somewhat greater. But the 35 hp are still enough for a top speed of 75 kph (46 mph)—an enormous figure, scarcely imaginable for the normal people of the time.

How resounding the success was had already been shown in Paris at the end of 1902. The fifth International Automobile and Bicycle Exposition had shown how essentially the automobile world had changed. Technical solutions in the Mercedes models, like high-performance radiators, lower center of gravity, and long, low silhouettes already

defined the standards. The French press stuck its finger directly in the wound: It called the show the "Mercedes Salon"—and called Wilhelm Maybach the "King of the Designers."

Thus the Mercedes 35 HP, in an era when there were no cinemas or airplanes, not only became the first of all supercars, but even the trendsetter for the basic development of the automobile. It was not only the first Mercedes and the first modern automobile, but also the first supercar in the world. What a shame that not one specimen has survived.

Technical Data

Make	Mercedes
Model	35 HP
Years Built	1901
Engine Type	in-line 4-cylinder, 5,913 cc (360 cu in), 26 kW (35 hp) at 950 rpm
Gearbox	4-speed toothed-wheel
Top Speed	~75 kph (46 mph)
Dimensions	wheelbase 2,620 and 3,020 mm (103 and 119 in)
Weight	1000 kg (~2,200 lbs) and up

Success Spurs Them On

The 35 HP proved to be far ahead of its competition. The Daimler-Motoren-Gesellschaft quickly added to this: With the 40 HP Simplex, Chief Designer Wilhelm Maybach consequently thought beyond his supercar design.

n the first years of the twentieth century, success followed success. The public and the experts were excited by the stunning success of the Mercedes 35 HP. In a very short time, Wilhelm Maybach's design awakened the automobile manufacturers who now had a master plan for the modern car. Suddenly there was a clear direction in which further development was to proceed: a sleek silhouette with a long wheelbase, an engine that ran quietly and yet released a lot of power, plus high-performance cooling and low weight.

Success spurred them on. The Daimler-Motoren-Gesellschaft did not stop, but soon produced two smaller sister models to the prominent 35 HP—and in March 1902 they registered the "Mercedes" name as a trademark. In the autumn of 1901 designers Wilhelm Maybach and Josef Brauner began to plan an adequate successor to their great gamble. The new topline model was the Mercedes-Simplex 40 HP, again a new idea, again a new, strong name: Simplex.

On the outside, Maybach left the engine almost unchanged. But inside the displacement increased to a proud 6,786 cc (414 cu in), the power to 40 hp. An important step, for their competitors from France were already moving a step forward in terms of performance. The designer now put a lot of stress on a carburetor that was technically improved. Maybach had also given more thought to the cooling system, which had gained much attention on the previous model. For the Simplex 40 HP he developed a flywheel with air-intake scoops, while omitting the radiator ventilator. Special ducts directed the air to the engine room, while metal sheets closed off the bottom of the car. Thus Maybach was setting new standards.

Forty horsepower for 942 kg (2,076 lbs) seems very sluggish today. In 1902 it was a clear promise: All the competitors are considerably heavier

Mercedes has an excellent reputation in racing. The Simplex 40 HP contributed to it. In this picture, Willie K. Vanderbilt is driving such a car in a (not very successful) race on the Circuit du Nord.

and they produce considerably less power. That pleased Emil Jellinek, particularly as he received the first car in March 1902—just at the right time for Race Week, which began shortly afterward. The winner of the Nice-La Turbie mountain race on April 7, 1902, was E. T. Stead in a Mercedes-Simplex 40 HP, just as the Mercedes 35 HP had won the previous year.

Unlike the Mercedes 35 HP, the 29 examples of which are completely gone, one authentic Mercedes-Simplex 40 HP can still be admired in the Mercedes-Benz Museum. It is surely not a Jellinek car, but its history is no less exciting. It is exactly the fifth car that the Daimler-Motoren-Gesellschaft built. As the oldest surviving witness, it reports directly on Maybach's brilliant designing. The car is also part of an episode that shows how excellently the Mercedes-Simplex 40 HP fits into this gallery of supercars.

Its buyer was William K. Vanderbilt, Jr., an auto fan and millionaire's heir from America. He already owned a Daimler Phoenix and a Mercedes 35 HP. The 24-year-old loves nothing more than passing his time in Europe with record runs and long-distance races. On March 14, 1902, Willie K., as friends call him, picked up his Mercedes-Simplex 40 HP, with a light racing body, in Cannstatt. With

The best-developed Mercedes met excited international customers. At the wheel sits E. T. Stead.

a companion and a mechanic, he immediately set out for Paris, arriving the next evening. That was an impressive achievement in 1902: more than 600 kilometers (372 miles) on small and smaller roads in the worst condition, struggling from town to town, with no gas stations, no road signs. For this run the mail coach needed a week. The young up-and-coming Vanderbilt loved exciting acts like this.

Stead drove a Mercedes-Simplex 40 HP at the Nice Racing Week. He won the Nice-La Turbie hill climb.

It looked quite harmless, but amounted to as much as an S 65 AMG 110 years later. At least!

Just a few days later the story went on. This time the finish was at Nice, 1,000 kilometers (620 miles) farther south. They drove over mountain passes, through rain and thick snowdrifts, without a top, for the racing body had none. On the way they are arrested, for a policeman accused them of speeding. That irritated the trio only briefly, and at 3:00 A.M. they fled from the police and drove on. Starting the car was a very demanding procedure that had to be mastered: With an air pump, about 0.3 bar (4.35 psi) of gasoline and oil pressure are built up on the instrument panel before the valve was opened, so the engine's lubrication points can be supplied with oil. But that took about five minutes and had to be checked in nine small glass indicators on the dashboard. The ignition had to be switched on, the choke lever was pushed forward, the decompression lever pushed, the spray-jet carburetor flooded. At the wheel, the levers were set for ignition, the mixture regulator and air level positioned. Only then comes the clockwise cranking—so it took time, skill, and strength before the engine finally ran. But all of that was no problem, Vanderbilt reported, not even in that nighttime flight, for "fortunately these 40 HP Mercedes are absolutely soundless."

Things went on adventurously. "After a few kilometers our way was blocked by numerous snowdrifts," Vanderbilt noted in his diary, "for which we had to make a running start several times before we plowed through them. At 6:00 A.M. the trio reached the small town of Serres, where they ordered their breakfast from an old lady in an inn. "I believe she thought we were patients fleeing from a madhouse, especially after we told her we had driven over the pass," Vanderbilt wrote further. "As far as she knew, nobody had tried it in the past five months, either with a car or a horse-drawn wagon."

Young, wild, and determined: Willie K. Vanderbilt at the wheel of his Mercedes-Simplex 40 HP.

Ex-Formula I driver and Le Mans winner Jochen Mass drives the Mercedes-Simplex 40 HP for the photographer.

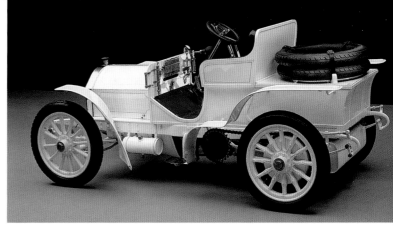

At 1:00 P.M. on March 20 they reached the finish line. Half an hour later they were in Monte Carlo. Several weeks later, on May 3, 1902, Willie K. Vanderbilt set out on a record run. He drove his Mercedes-Simplex 40 HP over a kilometer, with a flying start, on the road from Ablis to Chartres. His top speed was 111.8 kph (~70 mph), a new record for production cars, initiated and carried out by William K. Vanderbilt, who now joined Emil Jellinek as one of the best international Mercedes messengers.

But this Mercedes-Simplex 40 HP is also fascinating because its history is known completely to this day. In 1923 "Mercedes Joe," a racing mechanic who emigrated to America, took it over and used it to transport spare parts. The Scripps family of San Diego, who grew rich on newspapers, bought it in 1930. Their children learned to drive it. Later is served as a vehicle on the family's farm. In 1930 the Vanderbilt Simplex reached a hotel in San Diego before going into a Mercedes-Benz collection. It is the oldest existing Mercedes—and a typical supercar.

Technical Data

Make	Mercedes
Model	Simplex 40 HP
Years Built	1902–1903
Number Built	1,510 (all Simplex models)
Engine Type	in-line 4-cylinder, 6,785 cc (414 cu in), 30 kW (41.7 hp) at 1,050 rpm
Gearbox	4-speed toothed wheels
Top Speed	~80 kph (50 mph)
Dimensions	wheelbase 2,720 and 3,120 mm (107 and 123 in)
Weight	942 kg (2,076 lbs) and up

Pushing the Performance Envelope

Sixty horsepower performance is an enormous plus:
The performance of the Simplex 60 HP is 50% above its
predecessor. By a hairbreadth its success would have fallen
into the water: A big fire in the Cannstatt factory destroyed
completed Simplex racing cars.

uccess sets the mood. The Daimler-Motoren-Gesellschaft is on the right track with the right personnel and the right products at the beginning of the twentieth century. Even if there are personal problems, the most important parts fit.

Much of this is attributable to the influence of the merchant, artist of life, and auto nut Emil Jellinek, who, from his home in Nice, in southern France, set the model policy of the Cannstatt business. First as a dealer who took on a large part of the year's production, and from 1900 to 1909 as a member of the firm's board of directors. He has the best connections with the rich private owners, businessmen and nobles who gather during winter in the mild environment of the Cote d'Azur.

Jellinek's concept grew, the orders did not level off. Yet, so as not to lose touch with the apex, progress was needed—the competitors were not asleep. With great dedication the designers around Wilhelm Maybach worked on new models. In March 1903 the new Mercedes-Simplex 60 HP had already aroused great interest. It too, like its two ancestors, the Mercedes 35 HP and Mercedes-Simplex 40 HP, had a four-cylinder engine that—quite in the trend of the times—took on gigantic dimensions: 9.2 liters (560 cu in)

The design speaks a clear language: It is aimed at speed, sport and victory.

of displacement now allow 60-hp performance at 1,400 rpm. This development seems meager, but of course in 1902 it followed attainable logic: Since higher engine speeds were not yet attainable mechanically or thermally, the designers created the desired gain by increasing the displacement. It was as simple as that.

And as difficult. In the end, the engines got bigger and heavier all the time, a development that opposed the efforts to save as much weight as possible. Anyway, the displacement went up a respectable 14 percent from 6.6 to 9.3 liters. To raise the effectiveness of the cooling, the little pipes were given added flutings, which enlarged their surface area.

The Mercedes-Simplex 60 HP of Camille Jenatzy, winner of the 1903 Gordon Bennett Race.

Camille Jenatzy, the "Red Devil," shows no mercy and wins in Ireland.

Victory for number 4: Camille Jenatzy reaches 135 kph (~84 mph).

As was still customary then, various bodies were created for the different chassis-engine combinations. The technical basis proved to be unusually sturdy and reliable, and thus the 60 HP chassis was suitable not only for racing, but also as the ideal basis for comfortable driving; Mercedes wholesaler Emil Jellinek, for example, had a luxurious sedan body made. He used the formidable traveling limousine for family outings in the Maritime Alps and even drove from Nice to the family's other home near Vienna.

With a light, open racing body, though, ideal for a short-wheelbase chassis, the 60 HP Simplex becomes one of the world's fastest cars of its time. Spectacular racing success for the Daimler-Motoren-Gesellschaft is the result. Hermann

Braun, on April 7, 1903, at Racing Week in Nice, is able to reach an unbelievable 116.9 kph (~73 mph) in record runs on the famed Promenade des Anglais with a Mercedes-Simplex 60 HP—at that time the highest speed of any automobile with an internal combustion engine. The Nice-La Turbie hill climb is taken in a double victory by Otto Hieronimus and Wilhelm Werner, also with a 60 HP Simplex. But the triumph is not without tragedy: Count Zborowski, one of the ambitious gentlemen drivers of the Cote d'Azur, crashes fatally at the spot where Wilhelm Bauer met his fate three years before.

Another hard blow took place on June 9-10, 1903. In Cannstatt, a fire wiped out the assembly building of the Daimler-Motoren-Gesellschaft. Maybach's design bureau was destroyed, and so were over ninety partly finished cars—including three 90 HP racing cars prepared in detail for the Gordon Bennett race and already tested in April 1903. The new factory in Untertuerkheim was already being built, but by no means finished. Work went on there day and night, pushing hard. It was ready to begin production in December 1903.

But the renowned Gordon Bennett race was to take place in Ireland in only three weeks. Since the 90 HP racing cars could not be built in such a short time, the wires from Cannstatt to the world glowed. The Daimler-Motoren-Gesellschaft finally found a solution in the Mercedes-Simplex 60 HP owned by the American car enthusiast Clarence

G. Dinsmore. The multi-millionaire, who lived in France and was chauffered by ex-racing driver Wilhelm Werner, made his private 60 HP car available to the works after long negotiations.

Although the competitors already had cars with more than 80 hp, the Cannstatt folks wanted to try their luck—in 1900, 1901, and 1902 the Gordon Bennett races had taken place without German participation. Now, they finally wanted to show what performance the inventors of the automobile were capable of.

In Ireland the Belgian driver Camille Jenatzy went to the starting line for Daimler-Motoren-Gesellschaft. The "Red Devil," so nicknamed for his bushy red hair and his driving style, gained honors for his name: For an unbelievable 592 kilometers (~370 miles) he drove the 60-hp car expertly, yet safely, over the wretched roads, reaching speeds up to 135 kph (~84 mph) on timed sections. His average was 89.2 kph (55 mph) over six hours and 39 minutes! There were no problems.

Alas, what lender Clarence G. Dinsmore said about this magnificent job with his lent Mercedes-Simplex 60 HP, which was returned to him as the winner of the world's most important race of the time, was not recorded. Very probably he was, more than anything else, quite impressed by this supercar.

Technical Data

Make	Mercedes
Model	Simplex 60 HP
Years Built	1902–1905
Number Built	unknown
Engine Type	in-line 4-cylinder, 9,235 cc (560 cu in), 44 kW (60 hp) at 1,600 rpm
Gearbox	4-speed toothed wheels
Top Speed	~90 kph (~60 mph)
Dimensions	wheelbase 2,650, 2,750, and 3,745 mm (104, 108, and 147 in)
Weight	~1,300 kg (~2,870 lbs)

The successful Mercedes-Simplex 60 HP won several first places. Here Baron de Caters is seen at the start of the Paris-Madrid race in May 1903.

The Six-Cylinder Era Begins

While the personnel carousel at the Daimler-Motoren-Gesellschaft turned, the direction of its top models remained clear: The newly developed six-cylinder engine opened a new door in auto building.

n April 1907 a new era began for the Daimler-Motoren-Gesellschaft, for on March 31, 1907, Wilhelm Maybach left the firm. Again and again there had been disagreements between the leadership of the company and him, the "King of the Designers" and loyal comrade of the late Gottlieb Daimler. Now the trust had been so deeply shaken that the management finally forced a separation.

Other automobile manufacturers take careful note of the news. Maybach's departure pleases them. The Daimler-Motoren-Gesellschaft had separated from its most important and creative brain. Now the danger that threatened from Stuttgart-Untertuerkheim seemed fit to be overlooked. Emil Jellinek, the Mercedes wholesaler, Maybach-mentor, and member of the board, was angry at this step. In 1906 he had told one of the directors in a letter of the outstanding qualities of the chief designer: "Maybach, well-directed, is the greatest good luck for an automobile factory."

Now Maybach was gone. As his successor, the directors chose Paul Daimler, one of firm founder Gottlieb Daimler's sons. From 1902 to 1905 Paul Daimler, as technical director, already bore the responsibility for the branch factory in Wiener Neustadt. The directors gave him the critical job of reworking Maybach's designs, particularly the brand new and very modern 120-hp racing engine.

What remained of Maybach's legacy, this great designer and Daimler cornerstone, was his cars. Thus at first nothing changed in the running model program. The dependable engines remained in production. But Paul Daimler was able to set his own accent with his new 75-hp engine. For the design of the 10.2-liter (622 cu in) power plant went back to him. Parallel to it, a somewhat smaller version, displacing 9.5 liters (580 cu in) and producing 65 hp arose.

The hood grows longer; the six-cylinder engine needs space—and offers reserves.

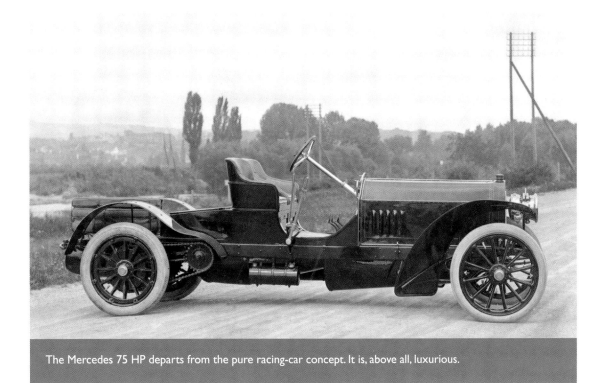

The Mercedes 75 HP departs from the pure racing-car concept. It is, above all, luxurious.

It has space. Its long chassis allows the 75 HP to carry all kinds of bodies. This is a landaulet from the stable of His Majesty, Kaiser Wilhelm II.

The innovative technology of the racing engine, as its problems show, is not yet ready for series production. Thus the engine of the Mercedes 75 HP still retains the cylinders cast in pairs. It also retains, as in the previous production cars, a side camshaft that operates the side intake and exhaust valves. Despite the traditional details, it has the new feature of being the first series-production Mercedes six-cylinder engine. The new model has dual ignition, not only by friction sparks but also by spark plugs. That sounds like an incidental note today, but back then the question of ignition that functions reliably in all running conditions was one of the central development tasks. The rear axle drive also retained chain drive.

The Mercedes 75 HP takes on the role of the top-of-the-line model at once. Thus it treads in the footsteps of the Mercedes-Simplex 60 HP. At first the Daimler-Motoren-Gesellschaft offers both models simultaneously.

It can be seen that at that time the ways parted permanently. In the first years of motorsport,

automobiles that were used in racing and competition were, as a rule, nothing but the highest-performance types of the regular model program. But from 1903 on the offerings varied. The firms, including the Daimler-Motoren-Gesellschaft, built not only production cars but pure racing models. The Mercedes 75 HP clearly took its side: It was a very sporting car, but it had nothing to do with entries in motorsports.

The new topline model of the Daimler-Motoren-Gesellschaft offered everything that would please the fastidious gentleman driver. The Mercedes 75 HP was not only strong and fast, but also expensive—just to own it, for the German financial authorities, required 3,120 Reichsbank notes from the owner for the right to operate a Mercedes 75 HP. That is a lot of money, representing about the yearly salary of a clinic doctor.

But that sum was not all; far from it. The costs of service and maintenance added up, and often a chauffeur was hired. On the road a host of expenses and tolls added up, charged everywhere by the authorities for driving on roads. There were impassioned protests against this by auto fans, speaking *en masse* against this extortion—even then. Leading them all was Prince Heinrich of Prussia, the brother of the German Kaiser, as a prominent lobbyist for the freedom of the auto driver.

These were not the only obstacles for the sport driver. Scarcely less problematic was the fact that at the time there were scarcely any roads in the German Empire that were adequate for the use of such an impressive car as the Mercedes 75 HP. It was also laborious for the driver to get suitable service for a breakdown or defect except in large cities like Berlin, Hamburg, Cologne, or Stuttgart.

Thus the customer, provided he had the financial resources, had many decisions to make before using his car. On the heavy, unbelievably solid, long-wheelbase chassis, very sporting open bodies with two or four seats could be mounted. The chassis also offered enough space for very classy bodies. The best example is Kaiser Wilhelm II, who had, among others, a Mercedes 75 HP landaulet in his motor park. Naturally, there were also closed touring cars suitable for summer holiday drives or promenades. They were as luxuriously fitted out as salons and offered all the fine features that could be put into an automobile in those days.

The first example of the 75 HP, as is documented, was delivered by the Daimler-Motoren-Gesellschaft to Nice—directly to Emil Jellinek, who had had so much influence on the firm's policies in the past years. He was rich and independent, and the possibilities of modern technology fascinated him: an ideal customer, and there were not many of them. In the end, as indefinite sources report, no more than 100 customers ordered a Mercedes 75 HP.

Those were other times.

Technical Data

Make	Mercedes
Model	75 HP
Years Built	1906–1910
Number Built	~100
Engine Type	in-line 6-cylinder, 10,180 cc (622 cu in), 55 to 59 kW (75 to 80 hp) at 1,300 rpm
Gearbox	4-speed
Top Speed	~95 kph (~60 mph)
Dimensions	wheelbase 3645 mm (143 in)
Weight	~1870 kg (4,122 lbs)

In the two-seater version, the 75 HP looks thoroughly sporty. That is all right with the customer.

The Pointed Radiator is the Latest Style

In Germany and Europe, the Mercedes 37/90 HP is not seen on race courses. In the United States it's very different. Here, among others, Ralph de Palma, with his engine tuned, drives from victory to victory.

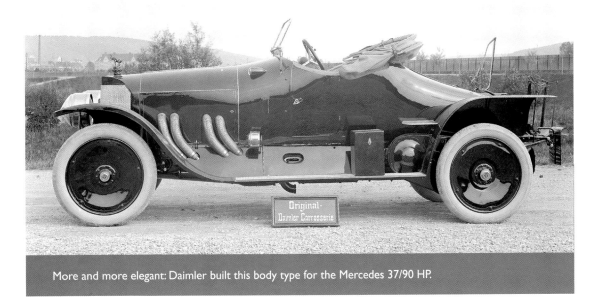

More and more elegant: Daimler built this body type for the Mercedes 37/90 HP.

The year 1911 was a long time ago. Connections and relations disappear in a gap of more than 100 years. What role did the automobile play a quarter-century after its invention?

For no fewer years lay between the first Benz Patent Motorwagon of 1886 and the brand new Mercedes 37/90 HP, which the Daimler-Motoren-Gesellschaft delivered from June 1911 on. The car had long since freed itself from the picture of the motorized coach. It took its own independent course.

The Mercedes 37/90 HP was the new topline model. Thus it replaced the 39/80 HP—the car that until 1909 was simply called 75 HP. Granted, the model names resemble each other as much as the cars themselves do from a present-day perspective. Particularly because the bodies often came not from the works, but from outside coachbuilders, they follow the trends of the times and the designer. Typical marquee designing was still not dominant in the years before World War I. One exception is the DMG, which founded its own body works in Untertuerkheim in 1906.

This four-seat touring body also came from the Daimler works.

Something more pleasing, even with a top: Daimler built bodies just as their customers wished.

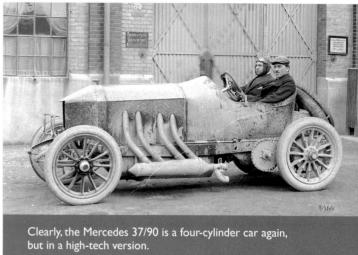

Clearly, the Mercedes 37/90 is a four-cylinder car again, but in a high-tech version.

The 37/90 HP is already a three-valve type.

But there was an essential difference between the new 37-90 HP and its predecessor. It represented the return of the Daimler-Motoren-Gesellschaft to four cylinders. Thus the first six-cylinder wave, that began in 1907 with the 75 HP model and its 10.2-liter engine, was over. That does not mean that it was simpler and more modest. Quite the opposite: The new four-cylinder engine sparkled with dual ignition and three-valve technology. Chief designer Paul Daimler, in charge since 1907, has designed another mighty big engine with a 9.5-liter (580 cu in) displacement. Performance came from volume; there was still no getting around that. The possibility of getting it by increasing engine speed will be allowed by technology only later.

Paul Daimler visualized one big intake valve and two smaller exhaust valves in the cylinder head. That allowed short gas ducts and thus good combustion. The valves were operated by a side camshaft, which was operated by gears that contacted the middle of the crankshaft.

The rear axle was still driven by a chain—for the last time in Mercedes history. This technology was chosen by the designers because it transmits high torque very reliably, much more so than a driveshaft did at that time. But even these old

familiar components could still be refined, as the Mercedes 37/90 HP showed: The driver chains ran in capsules and in an oil bath.

A minor improvement followed in the summer of 1913, when the Daimler-Motoren-Gesellschaft gave their models new names. The 73/90 HP became the 37/95 HP, and at the beginning of 1915—after successfully boring out to a 9.8-liter (~600 cu in) displacement—then the 38/100 HP. It was seen as a sporting, potent touring car with highly modern technology, usually ordered with open sports or racing bodies. Thus it was not a purebred racing car, nor a purely high-class car. One of the few 37/90 HP cars with a luxurious closed body was delivered by the Daimler-Motoren-Gesellschaft in 1912 to the king of Bulgaria. But most customers put more value on dynamics and cherished the sporty pointed radiator that already pointed the way to streamlining. The Mercedes was ahead of its time in that field. Only in the 1920s did streamlining become a popular theme. Typical of the sports cars from Untertuerkheim were the striking external exhaust pipes—only much, much later would they be wrongly interpreted as signs of a supercharged engine.

So the new Mercedes model offered many delicacies. Obviously, its price was as noble as its equipment; the chassis of a 37/95 HP alone cost 23,000 Marks in 1913.

How important the role of the automobile as a sporting article had become is shown by the growing numbers of events. In 1906 the Targa Florio was run as a demanding long-stretch race in Sicily, far away from all automobile factories. Motorsport became more and more fashionable, and in 1911, along with the production of the first 37/90 HP, the first runnings of two races still renowned to this day took place: the Monte Carlo Rally and the Indianapolis 500. Names that would become legends, just like the name of Juan Manuel Fangio, who was born in 1911 and would later become one of the best and most successful Formula I drivers of all time.

Less renowned today is the Vanderbilt Cup, named after Willie K. Vanderbilt, a millionaire's son and enthusiastic automobilist. In 1902, at the age of 24, he had picked up a Mercedes-Simplex 40 HP at the Cannstatt works and driven it to Paris and then to Nice. Back in America, he appeared as an initiator and sponsor of a race, that Vanderbilt Cup. In those days it was a very popular and respected motorsport event, first held on a road course in New York State—with the fastest and most powerful cars then on the market.

Mercedes, for example. The German marquee with the star on the grille was seen as an excellent choice, even though in terms of performance it had

The 37/90 HP appears strikingly slim and sporty with the "original Daimler bodywork."

competitors, including those made in America—but German manufacturers were successful too: Models of their competitor, Benz, also won numerous races in the USA.

Although the Daimler-Motoren-Gesellshaft was not actively involved in motorsport in those years, Paul Daimler accommodated the wishes of American Mercedes drivers: He had cars built based on the 1908 Grand Prix type and fitted them with Mercedes 37/90 HP engines. Unlike the extremely large original engines of Grand Prix cars, the three-valve model met the requirements for the Vanderbilt Cup and the Indy 500—in both races the displacement was limited to 600 cubic inches, equaling 9,834 cubic centimeters.

A dramatic finale in Indianapolis: Italian-American driver Ralph de Palma pushes his broken-down Mercedes over the finish line.

29

The American Grand Prize race, Milwaukee, 1912: The starting ranks full of cars.
Below: The Vanderbilt Cup, also in Milwaukee, a few days earlier. At the start, the third-place finisher, Spencer Wishart (No. 26), in a Mercedes. In a car of the same type, the "Gray Ghost," a 1908 Grand Prix chassis with a 37/90 HP engine, Ralph de Palma won the race.

In 1911 the Daimler-Motoren-Gesellschaft sent racing cars to the United States. One of them was received by one Spencer Wishart on his 21st birthday from his father, a successful Wall Street speculator. It was not Spencer Wishart's first Mercedes that ran in many races and gained success through much courage and some ability.

The second delivery from Cannstatt was bought by a lamp manufacturer from New Jersey. But this E. J. Schroeder, in his spare time the speed record holder for boats and the designer of an airplane, does not want to drive it himself. He prefers to play the role of the stable owner who leaves the diving to a pro. At the wheel is Ralph de Palma (1882–1956), a very charismatic, polished and successful American driver with Italian roots. The public—and his competitors—respect Ralph de Palma as a great sportsman. During his 25-year career he won an unbelievable 2,500 races (in which he used every possible means of earning)—and died, very unusual then for his line of work—not on the track, but of a natural death at the age of 75.

In 1911 Ralph de Palma first raced his new Mercedes, known to all as the "Gray Ghost" for its color and speed. In May 1912 de Palma and his "Gray Ghost" did not gain the best results but it was certainly the most sporting event of his career. He started in the Indianapolis 500, fought his way capably to first place on the third lap—and stayed there. He kept up an average speed of about 110 kph (~70 mph) and on lap 198 he led the second-place car by five laps.

Just over three miles from the finish (only a lap and a half), the 80,000 spectators in the grandstands are suddenly excited: Every car goes down the straight—except de Palma, who is suddenly missing. A technical defect has put him out of the running. His Mercedes engine has thrown a rod—the victory thought to be certain is gone. But Ralph de Palma is not one to give up: Along with his riding mechanic Rupert Jeffkins, he begins to push the heavy Mercedes. Tens of thousands cannot believe their eyes. And sure enough, the "Gray Ghost" crosses the finish line

Pioneer days of car racing: the "pit crew" with hubcaps and enthusiastic handiwork.

at a walk. Ralph de Palma and Rupert Jeffkins push the car into eleventh place. What they win is the greatest sympathy for their sporting efforts. Spencer Wishart, the rich man's son, drives his car of the same type to third place.

In August 1912 de Palma took two victories in Illinois in passing. Then on October 2, 1912, the 29-year-old started in the Vanderbilt Cup, held in Milwaukee, Wisconsin, that year. Even then motorsport was a traveling circus. Ralph de Palma won the Vanderbilt Cup easily, and Wishart again finished third. Just three days later came the "Grand Prize" on the "Milwaukee Mile." In this race things did not go so well: First, a young driver died in his Fiat, then de Palma collided seriously and skidded off the track. He barely survived and stayed in the hospital for two and a half months, until just before Christmas. There was one small consolation: He won the 1912 National Championship.

In February 1914, in the Vanderbilt Cup race in Santa Monica, California, Ralph de Palma won with his Mercedes "Gray Ghost."

Nineteen-fourteen was the next strong year for Ralph de Palma. The most important race was the Vanderbilt Cup, run on February 26 in Santa Monica, California. De Palma, as in 1913, was supposed to start as the chief of the American Mercer team. But many things go awry, and de Palma senses he is mistrusted. He withdraws his promise for 1914. Instead, just three weeks before the race, he asks his sponsor E. J. Schroeder again for the now aging "Gray Ghost." Schroeder agrees, which pleases de Palma. "My ancient beautiful race car," he lovingly calls the Mercedes.

The competitors, especially the Mercer team, do not take de Palma seriously. But what happened was a bold lesson in tactics and proved that boxing strategy is not a new invention, but could already

In the Sarthe Grand Prix in August 1913, one of the four Mercedes team cars had a 37/90 HP engine. With Leon Elskamp at the wheel, it finished in seventh place.

decide wins and losses in 1914. The drivers had to drive 35 laps on the 8.4-mile course, and when the race was half over, only four of the fifteen starters remained. Two fought each other for the victory: Mercer driver Barney Oldfield and Mercedes driver Ralph de Palma. Oldfield had already made two pit stops, while de Palma drove his Mercedes non-stop. Then he got an idea. Driving just ahead of Oldfield, he signaled, wildly gesticulating, to his pit crew that he would stop on the next lap. Then he let Oldfield pass him. He had seen de Palma's signal, and since his tires were worn down to their limit, he calmly stopped at his pit on the next lap.

But de Palma, just behind him, sped by. A trick! Oldfield saw that, accelerated out of the pits and fought bitterly for the just-lost lead. But he could no longer catch de Palma, who, thanks to his non-stop strategy, crossed the finish line some 200 meters (~220 yards) ahead of Oldfield. "That was the high point," de Palma said later; "That was the most exciting moment in the almost 30,000 miles that I have raced."

Technical Data

Make	Mercedes
Model	37/90 HP
Years Built	1911–1915
Number Built	unknown
Engine Type	in-line four-cylinder, 9,530 cc (580 cu in), 66 kW (90 hp) at 1,300 rpm
Gearbox	4-speed
Dimensions	unknown
Weight	unknown

It is scarcely a surprise that the Mercedes 37/90 HP and later the 38/100 HP models were successful in the United States. Ralph de Palma, the popular driver, and his noteworthy performances had a large share in the success. The series remained in production until 1915.

Ralph de Palma wins the 1914 Vanderbilt Cup in Santa Monica, California.

Victory in Sicily

On the distant island of Sicily, the Mercedes 28/95 HP scored great success. But this type made history for another reason, too. It was the first Mercedes fitted with a supercharger.

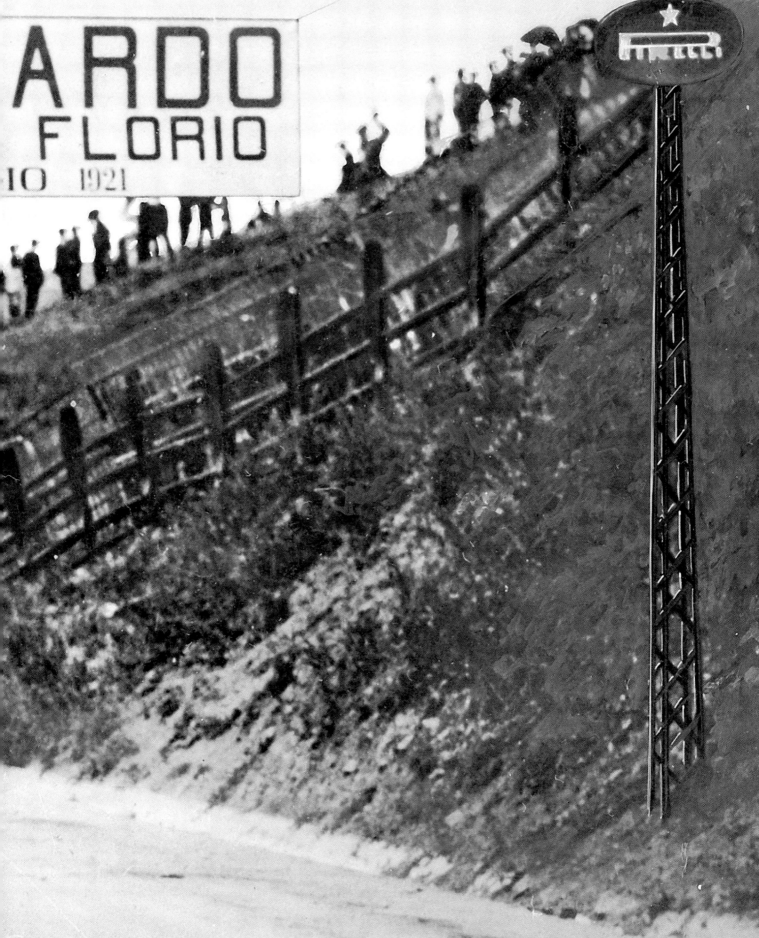

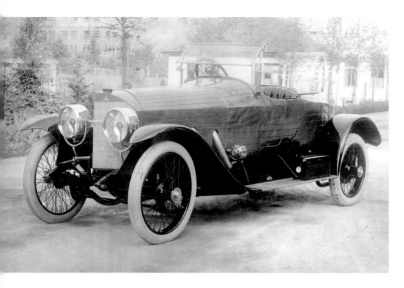

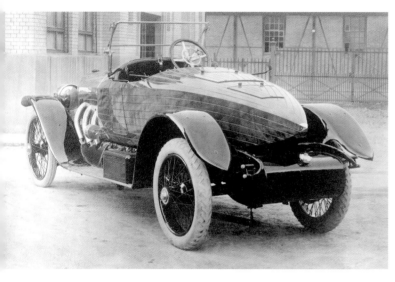

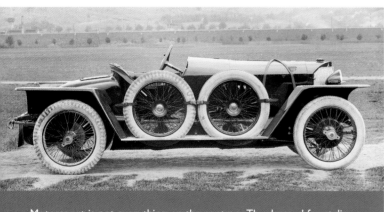

Motorsport is not everything; on the contrary. The demand for styling increases, as these notably stylish boat-tail bodies (above) and the angular roadster silhouette show.

Simply imagine: What would it be like to almost win the Targe Florio in 1921? That is not a race around the corner. It does not take place in a region whose language one speaks or whose infrastructure one can depend on. Targa Florio is held in Sicily, the last European outpost before Africa begins. Of course German Hohenstaufen emperors had been here before. But automobiles and drivers?

They actually came, even in the first decade of the twentieth century. The first Targa Florio, which took place in Sicily in 1906, was organized by the Italian industrialist and auto enthusiast Vincenzo Florio. It quickly became the most important sports car race on the international scene. There are scarcely any others. The Nuerburgring is not built yet, the 24-hour Le Mans not yet established, nor the Mille Miglia either. But this insane excursion through the bald mountains of the Madonie, in which a single lap covers more than 148 curving, dusty, bumpy kilometers, lures the best brands and drivers.

For example, Max Sailer. He is, like most racing drivers of his day, both a driver and a technician. Sailer is an employee of the Daimler-Motoren-Gesellschaft, but is better than others in both fields. For no other German can drive harder and wilder than he in 1921, nor faster. He first proved his ability in the legendary 1914 French Grand Prix. He did not take part in Mercedes' 1-2-3 victory because he threw a rod on the sixth lap—but that happened when he was leading by some three minutes. As annoying as the failure was, the honor was Sailer's, for he made the fastest lap of the race. But Sailer was not only capable as a driver. As an engineer, he also knew the theory behind the technology that he drove in excellent fashion. And even more: He could even work on it himself.

He applied his abilities to the Type 28/95 HP. This car was then the top Mercedes model, which the Daimler-Motoren-Gesellschaft had introduced in 1914. It was a car that broke the former limits. Instead of the chain drive formerly common in this performance class, it had a driveshaft that transported the power from the engine to the rear axle. And that easily did it all: The 7.3-liter (445 cu in), six-cylinder engine was based on the DF 80 aircraft engine with which the DMG had finished an honorable second behind Benz in the 1912 Kaiserpreis competition for the best airplane engine. Its design was very demanding for those times: The valves were dropped in V-shape and operated by an overhead camshaft via rocker arms. The drive was produced by a vertical shaft, a very rare feature in auto building. Two carburetors supply fuel to three cylinders each.

The engine is convincing as an extremely refined, solid, and potent power plant. At least the last two points are ideal prerequisites for use in motorsport, even if the engine seems unsuited

for high engine speed with only four crankshaft bearings. All the same, the top engine speed of the 95 HP is 1,800 rpm, an extraordinarily high value for those times. In comparison, the similarly expensive and superb Rolls-Royce Silver Ghost produced only 48 HP at 1,200 rpm from its similarly dimensioned engine.

Despite its potential, it was not put to use in racing at first. World War I breaks out in 1914, thoroughly ruining the plan to run this excellent car, which at 24,000 Reichsmark cost a great deal, on the graveled driveways of the steel barons, paper factory owners, or fine fabric dealers. Before the war, only 25 of the 28/95 HP were built.

The fast Type 28/95 HP was the first Mercedes with standard front-wheel brakes.

The Type 28/95 HP takes on a different appearance in light racing trim. Here it is loud and hostile.

Standard Front-Wheel Brakes Begin in 1923

as the foundation of grandiose, high-performance supercars.

Max Sailer got to work. The whole responsibility for vehicle development and motorsport participation in the DMG belonged to none other than Paul Daimler, son of founder Gottlieb Daimler and technical director of the firm from 1907 to 1922. Sailer began with the chassis and shortened the wheelbase a good 30 centimeters (~12 inches) from 3,370 to 3,065 millimeters (133 to 120 inches), moved the striking, stylish pointed radiator backward and mounted it more deeply. Also deeper: the driver's and mechanic's seats, and for this reason Max Sailer also had to make the steering column more level. The production brakes do not satisfy him either; the heavy car has to make do, in the style of the times, with two-wheel and driveshaft brakes. Max Sailer adds four-wheel brakes, a tremendous step forward. The brakes are still operated by cable, which was hard to adapt to the steered front wheels. As of 1923 the four-wheel brakes with their gray cast drums are made standard on the 28/95 HP.

Only in 1918, when Germany lay shattered after losing World War I, could the Daimler-Motoren-Gesellschaft slowly think of civilian production of the 28/95 HP. Slight technical changes ensued; for instance, the formerly free-hanging valves were now put under covers, and the cylinders, hitherto single, were now cast in pairs. Gradually it becomes evident how well the chassis of the 28/95 HP, along with its large-displacement, six-cylinder engine, was suitable not only as the basis of a mighty high-class touring car, but also

Max Sailer returns from Sicily with a win in the Targa Florio, driving his own racing car.

Left: Otto Salzer with mechanic August Grupp at the Untertuerkheim works after returning from the Karlsbad-Marienbad-Karlsbad spa race.

Obviously, it is hard work at the steering wheel of the 28/95 HP racing car. Otto Salzer with mechanic Grupp are seen at the Koenigsaal-Jilowischt hill climb in Prague in May 1921. Sailer would win the race.

Thus the 28/95 HP won the production-car class of the 1922 Targa Florio.

We do not know the details of all the modifications Max Sailer undertook. It is definite, though, that his cure was more than successful. The highest values recorded were 99 hp of power and some 130 kph (80 mph) of top speed.

As the "Mercedes 28/95 HP Sport" (or "Mercedes 28/95 HP Racing Version"), the supercar developed by Max Sailer was put on the market, as two- or four-seat tourers, as the buyer wished.

The 28/95 HP also played a special role as a test car as of 1920. The first tests with the Roots supercharger, already used with aircraft engines, showed what possibilities there were in supercharging car engines. But supercharged models of the 28/95 HP were not put up for sale.

The 28/95 HP was also the first model that appeared at the start of motorsport events after World War I. To be sure, it was not Max Sailer who sat at the wheel in the first race. At the Czech mountain race from Zbraslav (Koenigsaal in German) to Jilowischt, Otto Salzer set a new record on May 22, 1921, and drove his competitors into the ground. Just a week later came Max Sailer's triumph in Sicily. Before that—as a test driver, dealer, racing engineer and driver all in one—he had driven his 28/95 HP Sport from Untertuerkheim to Cerda himself, driving over the Alps and through Italy. Despite this strain,

Sailer, already 38 years old, drove four long laps, fought hard on miserable roads against strong opposition—and finally finished second on May 29, 1921. Max Sailer could have been satisfied with that, for he could still bring a trophy home to Untertuerkheim in his 28/95 HP Sport: the special "Coppa Florio" for the fastest production car in the race. And he did it with a car that was not developed for motorsports at all.

The first place went to Count Giulio Masetti in a Fiat. The Italian nobleman was so excited about the performance of the Mercedes that he made contact with the Germans. Because the Daimler-Motoren-Gesellschaft did not want to sign him as a driver, the wealthy Masetti took the reins in his hand. He bought himself a 1914 Mercedes Grand Prix racing car, had it painted red—and won the

Salzer and Grupp also won the Karlsbad-Marienbad-Karlsbad race in August 1921 in the same car.

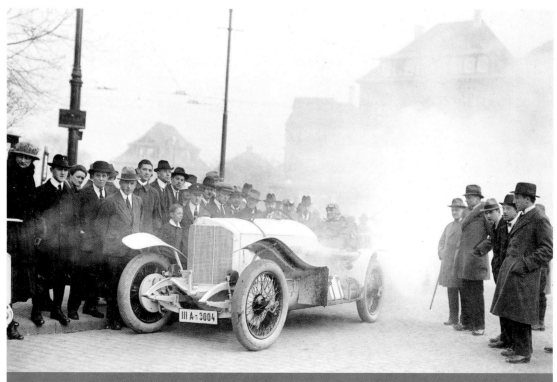

The adventure can begin: Christian Werner sets out on his own from Stuttgart on April 2, 1922, with his Mercedes 28/95 HP on his way to the Targa Florio in Sicily.

Honor to him who earns it: Heroes like Otto Salzer and August Grupp tell of their adventures.

1922 Targa Florio with it. Thus he, as a privateer, scored the first Mercedes victory in Sicily, even before the archrival Alfa Romeo. Max Sailer was there again, too, this time with a supercharged 28/95 HP Sport, which now produced 140 hp, and had an unbelievable amount of thrust in acceleration, and clearly exceeded 140 kph (87 mph). In his class, production cars more than 4.5 liters (275 cu in), Max Sailer won. In the over-all classification, though, that was only enough for sixth place. It was the first race in which Mercedes cars with supercharged engines started, for besides Sailer's car, the DMG also entered their new supercharged 1.5-liter (92 cu in) racing car. Masetti's winning car, on the other hand, was unsupercharged.

The racing career of the 28/95 HP Sport lasted until 1927. It won prominent races like the Coppa Acerbo as well as hill climbs—the "Hercules" in Kassel and the Semmering. In sprint racing as well, such as in Scheveningen, it gained spectacular success. To be sure, the winning drivers were all private owners. Among them, numerous Italian names were found. But this could scarcely matter, for it proved how widespread Max Sailer's Targa Florio success and Count Masetti's impressive demonstration had effect. At the start of the

1920s, motorsport was already seen as the ideal marketing instrument.

For Max Sailer, the time of adventures behind the wheel was then over. He went his way, step by step. Early in 1935 the engineer was chosen to be the technical director and a board member of the Daimler-Benz AG. He was responsible for the complete development of production and racing-car building—including the legendary Silver Arrows. His legacy remains the 28/95 HP Sport.

Technical Data

Make	Mercedes
Model	28/95 HP
Years Built	1913–1924
Number Built	573 (all versions)
Engine Type	in-line six-cylinder, 7,280 cc (444 cu in), 69 kW (94 hp) at 1,300 rpm
Gearbox	4-speed
Top Speed	130 kph (80 mph)
Dimensions	wheelbase 3,370 mm ([133 in] production), 3,065 mm ([120 in] sport)
Weight	1,260 kg ([2,777 lbs] chassis)

The Road to International Greatness

Mercedes-Benz, thus the new name since the merger, strives toward the top. With the 24/100/140 HP Model K, the supercharger becomes the exclusive cornerstone of the automotive luxury class.

Luxury in hard times: The supercharged car impresses the auto world. At the wheel of this one is Fritz Nallinger.

Now, for the first time things went on somehow. They scrambled up slowly, tried to get their political bearings. With the Weimar Republic, Germany tested, with no experience at it, the complex system of democracy. Politics and the economy sense how isolated Germany is; in wartime the chimneys smoke, producing as much as possible. Now industry is largely halted, and the structures break down like a house of cards. There are scarcely any raw materials or production, which means no work and thus no money to spend on the people. The government says they must do something and prints money, more and more money.

But this causes currency devaluation, which takes on a unknown and never-suspected dimension. Hyper-inflation breaks out across the land; its drama and brutality turn even apocalyptic fears to a farce. In 1923 it was so absurd that a liter of milk, which cost 1,500 Marks in mid-June, cannot be had for less than 240 billion Marks by the end of November. It is grotesque how the prices explode. Whoever gets his pay must go shopping at once—the next day the money is not worth anything any more. Many communities and many businesses, including the DMG, struggled with the currency, trying to remain stable. They tried for normality and only broke things along the way. Only at the end of 1923, when the Rentenmark came, and the Rehchsmark the next year, did the hyper-inflation end.

The beginning of the 1920s was not a time blessed with inner peace and relaxed riches. World War I, the first great disaster of the new century, was over. The German Empire had taken it on and had lost, although at the start they were so confident and madly sure they would win. They calculated wrongly. When the weapons went silent at the end of 1918, national pride was eroded. The Kaiser was gone, the Communists were going to the barricades, the Treaty of Versailles burdened the Germans with high reparations and caused much discouragement. The opponents of Germany wanted to make a clear example: It isn't done that way. Never again such a show that ended in such slaughter and such chaos.

Very civilian: The successful private driver Adolf Rosenberger in a Model K.

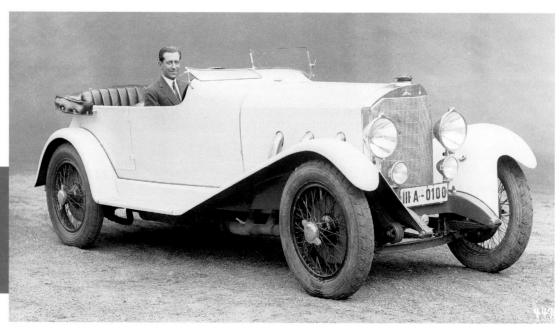

From the factory comes a markedly quiet and yet elegant body.

In unsure, unorganized, untested, and nervous times like these, many things are eagerly desired. Bread, for example, but also cigarettes, beer, and liquor, because they always functioned as currency and helped out when one ached all over. At such a time the Daimler-Motoren-Gesellschaft now presented the successor to the 28/95 HP, a new top-of-the-line model: the 24/100/140 HP. As a Pullman limousine it was best for business-, states-, and churchmen, and in 1926 it cost an unbelievable 27,750 Reichsmark; the tourer cost 23,800 Reichsmark, the chassis 19,250 Reichsmark. That was so much that it was not affordable even after a long lifetime of normal work.

One might call that courageous, perhaps also somewhat blind. And yet, the Untertuerkheimers made it, developed it farther, made it better, stronger, faster, more beautiful, as if there were no crises surrounding them. It was simply shielded, and in fact, it found some customers. They were hand-picked. Cars like the 24/100/140 HP were parked in the garages of Germany's loveliest villas, in Essen, Stuttgart, Hamburg, or Berlin. Here and there one of the old established noble families could free up enough money for luxury items like a car. In the United Kingdom in particular, the top Mercedes model enjoyed great admiration, but in America and Switzerland, too, the Daimler-Motoren-Gesellschaft sold the noble 24/100/140 HP. It was a picture of a car, big, strong, and self-assured, strong and capable, imbued with

conservative nobility and yet very modern in its design. Where the top Mercedes model rolled, respect, astonishment, and, as always, some envy prevailed.

Only for stars and entrepreneurs: The supercharged models play in the highest league.

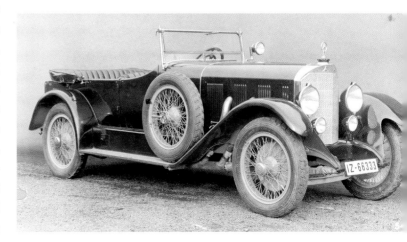

The Supercharger Comes from Aircraft Construction

The new type from Untertuerkheim unquestionably would have found more buyers in other times, despite its exorbitant price. After all, it offered a lot of car for the money. One cannot be on the road more royally from the end of 1924 on in anything but a 24/100/140 HP. The results of this code of three cryptic-sounding numbers still indicate, to those in the know, the technical concept that stands behind them. The 24 HP did not indicate its engine power, but rather the tax horsepower, which the financial authorities calculated on the basis of its engine displacement—261.8 cc represented one tax HP. The second number (100 HP) was the actual value of the nominal engine power. And the third figure (140 HP) finally showed how strong the car was when the supercharger, howling loudly, switched on at full throttle, was pressing more and more air into the carburetor.

The supercharger! This primeval power, howling when high performance is needed, came from a strongly ribbed, magical piece of technology that Daimler first tested in airplane engines. The mechanical compressing, as practice soon proved, brought a lot of extra performance. Paul Daimler, one of Gottlieb Daimler's sons and technical director of the Daimler-Motoren-Gesellschaft in Untertuerkheim since 1907, wanted to achieve that in auto production, too. It is not so simple, he soon learned, for while airplane engines ran under relatively constant parameters, burdens and engine speeds changed constantly in a car's engine. That made the use of this technology on the street a whole lot more demanding than in the air. But if it succeeded, not only would the engine performance increase, but so would the demand—and thus the sales.

Paul Daimler had tested some things. The superchargers loaded large and small engines, and he tested to see which combinations were practical. Thus at the end of 1921 the Daimler-Motoren-Gesellschaft already introduced the 6/20

With their great power, the new models leave practically everything behind them.

HP (1.6 liters) and 10/35 HP (2.6 liters), which went into production a year later as the more highly developed 6/25 HP and 10/40 HP types. At this time, as 1922 gave way to 1923, Paul Daimler moved to Horch in Zwickau. His successor was Ferdinand Porsche, who had come from Auistro-Daimler and, at the age of 47, was now in the service of the Daimler-Motoren-Gesellschaft as its chief designer and board member.

Porsche soon realized that small-volume engines did not harmonize ideally with Roots superchargers. Engines with bigger dimensions were better suited for supercharging, not because any performance was lacking at low engine speeds; that was not the problem. It dealt rather with the wish to be at the point of calling forth an extra portion of performance, for fast acceleration, for example, when passing. The supercharger seemed ideally suited for big touring cars, and also for racing cars. In 1923 the young, and still unknown, driver Rudolf Caracciola won his first race for Mercedes with supercharger technology. His racing car was a Mercedes 1.5-liter car built especially for racing, and

he drove it to victory at a hill climb in Muennerberg, Lower Franconia.

Ferdinand Porsche, the new design chief, maintained an impressive tempo. He designed two, six-cylinder engines, a 4.0-liter type that went onto the market as Type 15/70/100 HP, and a larger version with 6,240-cc (380 cu in) displacement, which powered the 24/100/140 HP top model. Both were supercharged and appeared, not too far apart, in the autumn of 1924.

As with the 28/95 HP model, the finest technology was behind the impressive, mighty, even façade of the engines. The camshaft was up in the head and was driven by a vertical shaft—a genuinely precise, reliable (and economical) solution. The material, silumin, was a modern light-metal alloy containing silicon; Porsche had engine blocks and valves cast of it. Even the pistons attracted attention, being made of aluminum, which of course was given a hard outer layer. Everything about this new car was laborious and expensive. The noble technology added its share to the exorbitantly high price of the 24/100/140 HP.

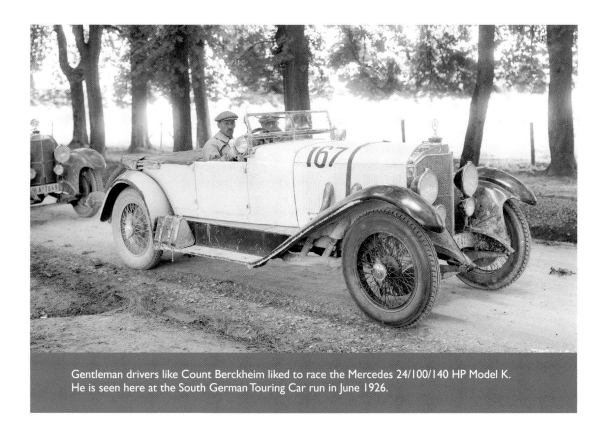

Gentleman drivers like Count Berckheim liked to race the Mercedes 24/100/140 HP Model K. He is seen here at the South German Touring Car run in June 1926.

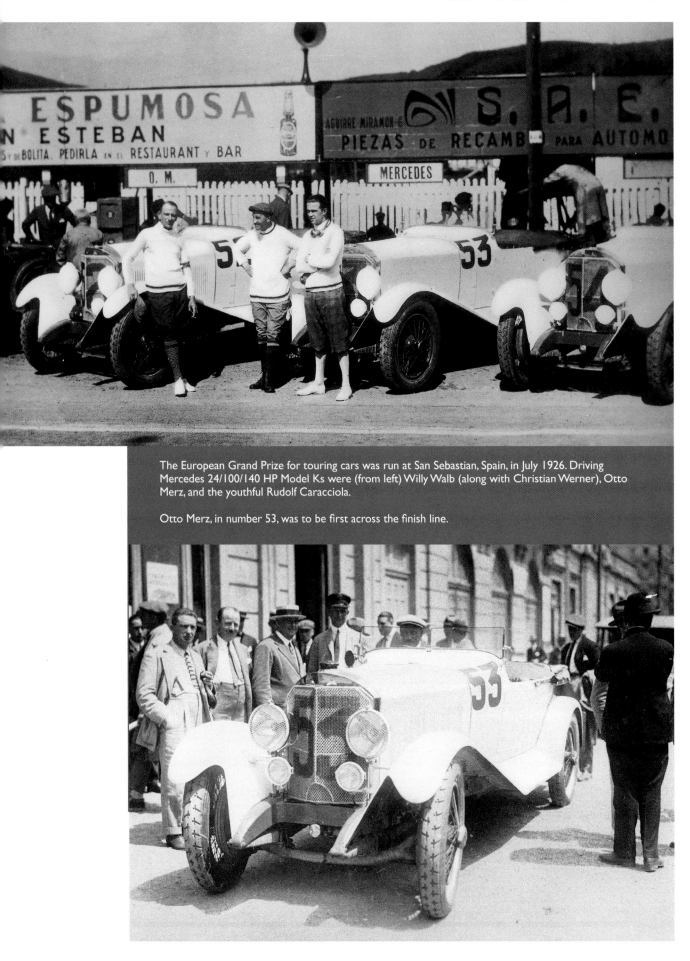

The European Grand Prize for touring cars was run at San Sebastian, Spain, in July 1926. Driving Mercedes 24/100/140 HP Model Ks were (from left) Willy Walb (along with Christian Werner), Otto Merz, and the youthful Rudolf Caracciola.

Otto Merz, in number 53, was to be first across the finish line.

Caracciola's (front) supercharged Mercedes and Merz's (back) were admired by spectators.

It was a lot of performance that the car produced with just a single carburetor. Despite an empty weight of about 2.5 tons, it was enough to get the car's speed up over 120 kph (~75 mph), depending on the rear axle ratio. In the first half of the 1920s, when superhighways were still distant utopias, one may ask where one was supposed to drive 120 kph. On the dusty, curving, narrow country roads? On the slippery, bumpy paved roads between horse-drawn wagons, handcarts, chickens, and pedestrians? But that was not the question that arose. The task that Ferdinand Porsche took on was different: He wanted to design a car that would show the apex of the possible again. He wanted to turn the technologically doable into technology. The new Mercedes should excite with its progress, without for a moment raising the suspicion that it is just unreal play. "It is the distinguished, proper car for city use, like the thoroughbred fast car for a big trip, the monarch of the highway," prospective customers read in a carefully composed catalog.

What was possible with the 24/100/140 HP was shown by Rudolf Caracciola in the Robert Batschari Tour in 1925. After almost 2,000 kilometers (~1,243 miles) on the road, the driver, later to be a star Grand Prix driver,

won. Sporting events went on. In May 1926 the Daimler-Motoren-Gesellschaft put the "6-Liter Mercedes Model K," a sporting variant of the 24/100/140 HP, on the market. The letter "K" stood for "Kurz" (short), not for "Kompressor" (supercharger), as is often thought today—for the long version had a supercharger. Three striking (and potent-looking) exhaust pipes with gleaming ribbed metal jackets pushed proudly through the right side of the long engine hood—on the street they were admiringly called "supercharger tubes." The engines also differed slightly in technical terms from the versions installed in the long standard chassis: They had higher compression, dual ignition, and a six-bladed fan to improve engine cooling. Yet the performance stated in the type designation was corrected only in 1928, when the top sport model was called 24/110/160 HP Model K.

Shortening the wheelbase by 35 centimeters (from 3.75 to 3.40 meters [~12 to 11 feet]) guaranteed clearly better handling. For the longer version required hard work on curves. Despite all the progress, it was not for the weak. It was not a problem; the longer standard models were driven only by trained chauffeurs—the rich folks rode in back. They didn't speed on curves.

51

Excitement before the start at San Sebastian. The Mercedes team cars are the favorites.

In the Model K, this agile, short, 50 kg (110 lbs) lighter version of the 24/100/140 HP, things were a bit different. Whoever bought it had sporting ambitions. He drove it himself, liked to have a young lady at his side, and had enough time and money to enjoy the sunny side of life. For their summer vacation they drove to their country estate, to Baden-Baden or Bad Homburg, to the casino. Relaxation instead of burdens, but with style: noble young bachelors and amateur racing drivers, gentlemen drivers, were the clientele that the firm tried to lure in a brochure: "Sit at the wheel of this car, feel the forward rush, the breathtaking speed of 145 kilometers per hour, the splendid power of the supercharged engine, but also the safety, the quiet stance on the street, the obedience of the brakes, the playful lightness of the steering." This car could do it all.

Indeed, for in 1926 a Model K won the prestigious Klausen Hill Climb, but with Caracciola at the wheel. At the Semmering he won the "Grand Mountain Prize of Austria." There were countless victories in the popular "automobile competitions," speed tests and reliability runs of the time. Racing and touring cars were all the same: "This model equally unites two cars into one!" a brochure lauded.

Nothing is Faster than the Model K

In the demanding Austrian Alpine Tour of 1928 as well, which led almost 2,300 kilometers (~1,430 miles) across mountain passes, the K models were convincing, with best times in all five stages. "Thanks to the fabled reliability of the machine, a playfully achieved sporting task," wrote participant Dr. Krailsheimer to the factory. W. R.

Wittlich of Darmstadt, who won the Alpine Cup for lone drivers, also praised his Model K: "Not long ago I made a trip through France and Spain, 5,000 kilometers (~3,107 miles) in all, with long daily drives, again without the least problem."

In 1926, shortly before the Model K was put on the market, something fundamental happened. At the end of June, the two best-known German automobile makers merged: Benz & Cie. and the Daimler-Motoren-Gesellschaft with their Mercedes brand. In times of crisis and weak markets, the two bitter rivals had already become partners in 1924, when the two firms approached each other in a mutually beneficial association. In 1926 it is confirmed. The new firm was called Daimler-Benz AG; the cars now bore the name Mercedes-Benz.

The still stronger Mercedes-Benz 24/110/160 HP Type K was the world's fastest production car of its time. "For the 6.3-liter car, with its 110/160 hp is the ideal vehicle to arouse a sporting spirit, always being the first, always the fastest." Thus the Mercedes-Benz catalog read. "Not without reason for the best-known international-class gentlemen drivers of this unique car."

Four brakes, not taken for granted in those days, were standard on the Model K from the start. As of 1928 even a brake-enhancing air intake supported the driver's work. And the 24/100/140 HP was given a meaningful type designation: After the tax-horsepower era in Germany ends, the car was also called the 630—representing its engine displacement divided by ten. The four-liter model, following this logic, was now the 400. Despite the economically very serious times, the variety of models increased. As of the end of 1928, Daimler-Benz offered the powerful 24/110/160 HP engine, also called the K engine, in the long chassis, too, where it helped to speed up the often-heavy tourer or Pullman varieties adequately. Powerful customers could now choose from six factory bodies, including a superb four-door convertible. What was even finer was to have a body for the bare chassis made by an expert firm. Great names were found here, the list running from Castagna through Satouchik to Erdmann & Rossi, plus

Deutsch, Baur, & Glaeser. In those days uncounted riches could scarcely be spent more impressively than on one of these great cars. The Model K was no longer produced at that time—even more powerful, successful and impressive supercars have appeared in its place.

The Model K could not be a sales success, for there were too few potential buyers. Yet it glowed in automotive history, standing for the beginning of the supercharged era, a technology that would celebrate its rebirth in new interpretations many decades later. The model name of the Type 630, the displacement divided by ten, is still valid today as a type designation. But much more important was its role as a forerunner, which it played for several generations of sports cars: The 24/100/140 HP Model K was the basis for the origin of the legendary S, SS, SSK, and finally SSKL.

Technical Data

Make	Mercedes-Benz
Model	24/100/140 HP Model K
Years Built	1926–1929
Number Built	395 (all types)
Engine Type	in-line six-cylinder, 6,246 cc (380 cu in), 74 kW (100 hp) at 2,800 rpm (supercharged: 103 kW [140 hp] at 3,100 rpm)
Gearbox	4-speed
Top Speed	~145 kph (~90 mph)
Dimensions	wheelbase 3,400 mm (~134 inches)
Weight	2,000 kg ([~4,410 lbs] chassis)

Premiere on the Nuerburgring

The theme of sport—"S"—constantly gains power for Mercedes-Benz.

In the new Model S, it consolidates as a high-performance "Sport" car

on the world stage.

For sport drivers, the agile car with the cumbersome name was very popular in the mid-twenties: the 24/100/140 HP Model K was a grandiose car, and is also known as the fastest touring car of its era. It was powerful, reliable, and successful—the chosen direction proved to be worth gold for Daimler-Benz. The successor, which chief engineer Ferdinand Porsche prepared for 1927, should fit perfectly into this groove.

The new model was called Mercedes-Benz Type S. Although Porsche had developed it as a high-performance sports car for racing, it appeared as a production car on the price list of the Mercedes-Benz sales program. The letter "S" stands for Sport, of course, a subject that became more and more important for Mercedes-Benz. This initial was more than just a chance choice, for the associations reach deeper. "Its name says it: Style and speed and victory," appears in text that the Literary Department of the firm wrote for the press in March 1928. This initial has never lost the significance of the special, even though it was to live on in another field decades later; the type letter first used in 1927 is firmly anchored in the S-Class today.

The Mercedes-Benz Sport, as the factory called its new model, was the second step in a series of model generations that made a big name in the automotive world from the Type K

A lot of passing prestige: Whoever sees the Type S like this, pulls aside.

into the thirties. The quintet of the Model K, S, and the following SS, SSK, and SSKL still make an impression today: Their exciting drama remains without an equal in automotive history. Whether the German Grand Prix, the Avus or Eifel races, the Tourist Trophy, the Mille Miglia or the 24 Hours of Spa, on and on—and an endless string of hill climbs—the list of S series victories alone is enormous.

A sports car of the international type, for the road and the race course.

No wonder that the Type S appeared deliberately as an independent model, all the more so than was the case for its predecessor, the K. K and S were obviously closely related. But if one looks at the details, much progress is seen—for example, in the chassis. Ferdinand Porsche, who worked passionately on the sports car, wanted to make the successor to the K tangibly faster and livelier. The way to that, as Porsche saw it, was a noticeably flatter body silhouette. His goal: The center of gravity must be moved farther down and also farther back.

To mount the body lower than before, Porsche had trimmed back the frame members considerably in the area of the axles. The results were clear, for now the chassis profile between the front and rear axles was clearly closer to the road. He also moved the engine back some 30 centimeters (12 inches), where it could be mounted lower and give a clearly better weight distribution. The pointed grille was also on the drawing board for modifications. It was made five degrees flatter than before and was also mounted farther back. As a result, the designers around Ferdinand Porsche also took the path to lighter construction; pierced cross members saved weight without hurting their function.

The Type S entered racing very sportingly. It set trends while also following the styles of its time by playing all sorts of aerodynamic tricks. For example, the driver could fold back the windshield of the S for streamlining in two steps, more handily than in the Model K. Even the front license plate could be folded flat. It was especially impressive that the headlights could be turned inward 90 degrees. Then the two big glass surfaces did not cause wind resistance. All of that was to help raise the final speed, the theory said. Whether these tricks actually gave measurable results is not recorded. But surely a driver of an S found great pleasure in measuring, with their stopwatches, the seconds and kilometers per hour gained from better streamlining. And psychologically it had a very positive effect. Just the aesthetics achieved by this tuning made any opponent worry.

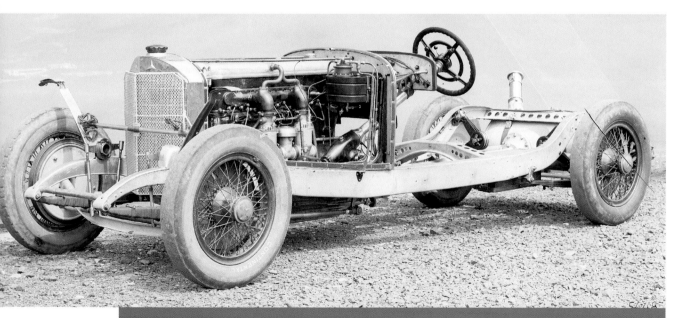

Under the sheet metal is the most modern technology of the twenties.

In any case, the new S was clearly faster than the K. The engine, bored out to 6.8 liters (~415 cu in) contributed much to this, even though this measure sounds simpler than it actually was. The two chief technicians, Ferdinand Porsche and Hans Nibel, who was once the chief designer for Benz & Cie., now chose wet instead of dry bearings. They also installed a new camshaft with optimal control times and fitted valve lifters. It was still—as a technical delicacy—driven by a vertical shaft. The result was a proud 120 hp at 3,200 rpm, but the performance data measured at full throttle with the supercharger running were really astounding. Then 180 hp with immense pressure briefly pushed the Type S ahead. From these data the car received its second, unofficial name: 26/120/180 HP.

The available power was enough to allow the Model S an easy sprint at more than 160 kph (~100 mph), at least as long as a light sport body was mounted and the driver was not afraid to let the wild Roots blower howl madly. With intensive use of this power reserve, of course, more than 30 liters (~8 gallons) of gasoline per 100 kilometers (62 miles) flowed out of the tank toward the carburetor. But since the tank held 120 liters (~32 gallons), a fueling stop was needed only at about 400 kilometers (~250 miles). Whoever drove his Type S in that style also learned soon how hard the car had to work for it; it became so warm that passengers felt as if their feet were resting on a grill.

Ralph de Palma drove the giant to two victories in 1928 races.

57

This is how the car that won at Nuerburgring in 1927 looked.

The Type S performed grandly at its premiere. It was June 19, 1927, when it appeared in public the first time. At the opening race of the Nuerburgring, which thousands of workers had stampeded out of the Eifel Mountains in just two years, teammates Rudolf Caracciola and Adolf Rosenberger started in Type S cars. The race on the "mountain, racing, and testing track" ran for 360 kilometers (~225 miles), and at the end the two Mercedes-Benz drivers raced across the line in first and second places before 85,000 spectators. Caracciola, the winner, was an astounding 17 minutes ahead of Rosenberger; no wonder his average speed of 101.1 kph (~63 mph) on the curving hill and valley road, with its 89 left and 85 right turns, was seen as the must astounding record. There was even a third Mercedes-Benz—a private Type K—in third place.

The variety of body types was vast. This body was built by Papler.

Technical Data

Make	Mercedes-Benz
Model	Type S
Years Built	1927–1930
Number Built	174 (all types)
Engine Type	in-line six-cylinder, 6,789 cc (414 cu in), to 140 kW (190 hp) at 3,000 rpm (supercharged to 184 kW [250 hp] at 3,300 rpm)
Gearbox	4-speed
Top Speed	~190 kph (118 mph)
Dimensions	wheelbase 3,400 mm (134 inches)
Weight	1,270 kg ([~2,800 lbs] chassis)

In the Grand Prix of Germany, which was run on the Nuerburgring only a few weeks later, a Type S also won. This time Christian Werner was at the wheel and drove the car's fastest lap at a speed of 107 kph (~67 mph). Just a little later, a Type S attains 177.4 kph (110 mph) in a race at Freiburg, and in Antwerp the sport model even reached an average speed of 194.6 kph (120 mph) in a sprint race. With victories at the Klausen and Semmering hill climbs, and even in the United States, it went on winning. Typical of the S, every weekend ambitious private owners scored new victories and speed records for Untertuerkheim. Among them, following the style of the twenties, were several women, including Ernes Merck of Darmstadt.

The privateers often used their racers as everyday cars during the week, for driving in the city and country. The Type S, despite its power and spirit, still was seen as a remarkably sturdy, long-lived, and reliable car. No car of its era was more successful, and no other offered such a brutal push

out of a low speed. In the city a Mercedes-Benz S rolled along easily in fourth gear. Thus shifting was not necessary. And even when it was rolling along at 1,200 rpm, barely over an idle, that was deceptive. It was not dozing, but lurking. The orgy might break loose at any second—and then there was no stopping.

The Type S was in production since April 1927, first parallel to the still-available earlier Type K. Mercedes-Benz tried in its November 1928 price list to show how different their characters were: The Model K was "the especially fast touring car of the pampered gentleman driver," the text stated, while the model S could be portrayed as "the world-famous super-sport model, the fastest sports car in the world."

The new "Special Supercharged Model S Sports Car" cost an incredible 30,000 Reichsmark. For this sum, Mercedes-Benz also delivered, as a substitute, four entry models of Type 8/38 HP—in any case, compared with other manufacturers—with two-liter engines. Thus the Type S cost some

The starting grid at the opening race on the Nuerburgring, June 19, 1927, with Mercedes-Benz monopolizing the first row. From left, Caracciola (#1), Rosenberger (#2), Rittmeister von Mosch (#3). They finished in the same order.

The main railroad station at the Uertuerkheim works. After his victory in the German Touring Car Grand Prix in July 1927, Otto Merz and his four-seat Mercedes-Benz S Sport were suitably received.

4,000 Reichsmark more than its predecessor. From the factory, Daimler-Benz offered the S as a luxurious touring car or convertible, in which four or more people found room. They all looked convincingly elegant: It was this layout with a low belt line that stood for pure sportiness along with the seemingly endless long engine hood. "Slim, stretched and fast as an arrow," as the Literary Department praised the design. For 26,000 Reichsmark the customer also received, if he/she wanted, a ready-for-use Type S chassis; then he could have the body built by a coachbuilder of his choice, just as he wanted it.

The victories won by the Type S kept on adding up happily. There were 53 first places and 17 records just in 1928. Daimler-Benz exported the fast Model S to Switzerland and Britain, Spain and Italy, France and the United States. The car, which

was also called the 680 S because of its 6.8-liter displacement, quickly grew into an automotive legend, although the numbers made were modest; in 1927 and 1928 a total of 146 were built.

The Type S was seldom seen on the road. But it was universally known, as the interest in car-show visitors shows; for instance, at the Geneva Automobile Salon in the spring of 1928: "Our stands, on which we showed this model," the Literary Department reported, "were constantly heavily surrounded, sometimes even stormed." And a journalist from the Netherlands was very impressed by a test drive in the spring of 1928, and told his readers: "Seat yourself in such a thunder-wagon, drive, fly with it, and you'll live differently! Your blood prickles in your veins like champagne, and you feel an uproar brewing inside yourself."

The Joy of Performance Gains

A fair amount of more performance and luxury made the Type SS one of the most desirable supercars of its time. It puts almost everything in the shade on the race course, just as on the boulevard.

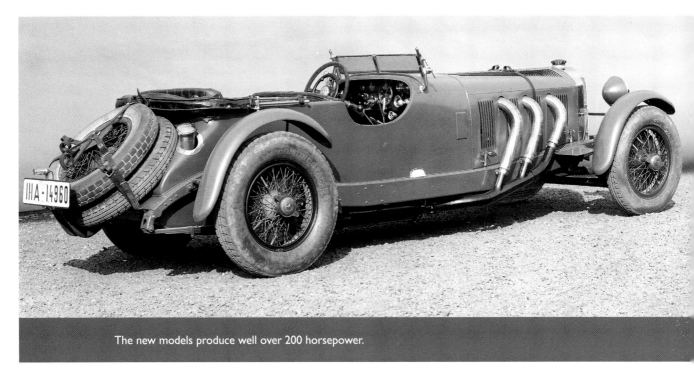

The new models produce well over 200 horsepower.

The success of the Model S took wing. It was not the mere numbers that pleased the Daimler-Benz directors; high numbers cannot be attained with an exclusive sporting vehicle like this. But the enthusiasm of customers from all over the world, the praise of motorsportsmen, and not least, the press, gave the feeling in Untertuerkheim that they had chosen the right path. The Mercedes-Benz brand enjoyed the highest admiration and renown, and not just in the established circles of rulers and nobles, dandies and heirs, but also the *haute volee* of sport drivers.

Daimler-Benz wanted to serve this potential clientele. Nothing was easier when there was a chance to build on a strong model like the Type S. The main requests that the new model was to fulfill sounded as simple as effective: more performance, more torque, more agility. It could be done, but something in the technology had to change. At first, technical chief Ferdinand Porsche had the bore enlarged another 2 to 100 millimeters, giving a displacement of 7,065 cc (431 cu in)—hence the occasionally used other name of Type 710. The pistons no longer had cast layering, but were made completely of aluminum. Larger valves provided better gas change for the long-stroke engine, and the four-bearing crankshaft

profited from a swing damper. In the gearbox, gears 1 to 3 were given longer ratios.

Nominally, the SS, the mechanics promised, produced a mighty 160-200 hp. But in practice the sport engine went over the magic 200-hp border when the supercharger came in at full throttle. The push was impressive, especially because it came in without increasing the engine speed. It came like a gigantic hand that pushed the car forward with unexpected power. The huge rpm gauge in the well-equipped instrument panel went up to 4,000 rpm. Daimler-Benz deliberately chose a lower engine speed. "In comparison with racing engines turning at 6,000 to 8,000 rpm, our SS sport models with 3,200 rpm at most can be called low-speed machines," a press release stated. "Spark-plug problems, the greatest weakness in high-performance engines, are unknown to our engine." There were other versions available from the factory running on special gasoline-benzol mixtures. Racing camshafts and superchargers were available on request for racing use. Then the performance climbed to 225 hp.

The manufacturer also explained the function of the supercharger. "In general, one will need the supercharger only to reach the desired touring speed more quickly, in order to go on without the supercharger," Daimler-Benz informed the Type

On the Nuerburgring the Type SS feels at home. It wins race after race.

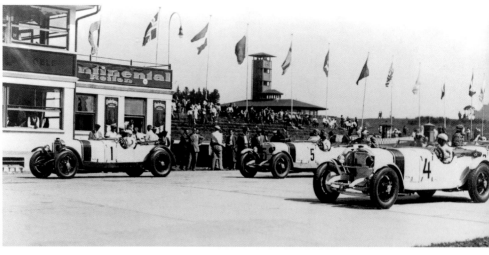

SS customer. And they do not request extra care in so doing: "No matter what gear is engaged, the supercharger may be turned on at any time." That was comforting. For there were rumors around that the supercharger would last the lifetime of the engine. They do not, Daimler-Benz promises. Everything has been made so lavishly that there can be no doubt of its durability.

It Carries Its Character in Its Name: Super Sport

The fact is that the supercharger lured. There was something illicit about it, something of anarchy that through the rationale of a solid development, as that of the Mercedes-Benz Type SS doubtless was, gained a specific charm again. Like a lady of

the best class with a slightly amorous reputation, perhaps. Such mixtures could lead one astray.

But the overworked Super Sport was not yet to be had. In the early summer of 1928 the first engines ran. The tested and dependable chassis of the Model S was to be kept. The new car was now called "SS", an abbreviation for Super Sport. It was the first Mercedes-Benz that actually had this term in its name.

These letters indicate its true character. In a hill climb on the Buehlerhoehe near Baden-Baden, the brand new SS started, still incognito, with Rudolf Caracciola at the wheel—who with this pre-series SS, still called a Type S, easily won all three special tests. Only two weeks later, on July 15, 1928, the first official appearance of the Mercedes-Benz Type SS ensued, under

Christian Werner in his Mercedes-Benz Type SS is flagged in as the winner of the 1928 German Touring Car Grand Prix.

the direction of the former driver and Porsche assistant Alfred Neubauer, now promoted to become racing manager. Four SS started in the German Grand Prix on the Nuerburgring, limited to sports cars. One of the cars went off the track on the second lap. But the success was overwhelming—Mercedes-Benz won the duel with Bugatti. The first three cars that crossed the finish line were white Mercedes-Benz Type SS. In many other races in the summer of 1928, the new top models from Untertuerkheim were right out in front. They were also very reliable; retirements from technical defects—other than tires—were unknown.

In October 1928 interested parties finally found it in the official price lists, where its predecessor, the Type S, still remained until 1930. The latter was no longer built, but Daimler-Benz sold the remaining ones that were left even though there was only a total of 146 built.

In races the SS ran in the sports car category, and sometimes also as a touring car. But the tremendous economic crisis at the end of the 1920s claimed victims. The manufacturer no longer took part in motorsports. Instead of company entries, the many national and international victories of the Type SS were all won by private entrants from the broad ranks of gentleman drivers. Outstanding was the victory in the Tourist Trophy in August 1929, which Rudolf Caracciola claimed for himself. The race ran for 660 wild kilometers (410 miles) and made demands on men and cars. Caracciola used every bit of performance in his SS; his average at the end was over 117 kph (~73 mph).

Yet in comparison with the Type S, the character of the SS developed another step away from racing. It pointed more strongly in the direction of *Gran Turismo*. As a fast touring car, it lured with its very sporting attitude but was ready to compromise just a bit. Only at the first moment could this situation be surprising. But development in auto racing went on, as did the customers' requirements in comfort, luxury, and renown. All in one? This was too extreme, and so the tendency to travel in two directions grew. That would last only a few years, until the professional racing cars would have nothing more to do with production models. For gentlemen drivers, that class of sportsmen who still had enough money for their exciting hobby and liked to go to the races on weekends, models like the Mercedes-Benz Type SS were just what they wanted: A car with which one could win. A car in which one's wife would also be happy to ride. Presumably because she will never experience the true sporting potential of the car.

Concentrating hard, Otto Merz drives his SS on the course of the 1929 International Tourist Trophy.

She will be especially happy to do it if he chooses the right body color from the array that Daimler-Benz offers for the SS. Since it, unlike its predecessor, the Type S, has a somewhat higher radiator grille, comfortable bodies with higher belt lines can be achieved. At first, though, there is just an open sports four-seater, which is joined in 1929 by a four-seat cabriolet. Later the SS is also available as a roadster and a special two-seat cabriolet. "For the paint and upholstery, various tasteful choices of color combinations, selected by artists, are available," the Daimler-Benz catalog reads.

The low production numbers are clear. The SS is so exorbitantly expensive that almost nobody can afford it. The most expensive version, the big cabriolet, costs an incredible 44,000 Reichsmark. Of course Daimler-Benz does not skimp on extra wishes: "Wishes concerning special equipment and non-standard fittings are largely accepted without extra charge," the catalog proclaims. And the SS shows itself to be lavishly appointed in the production versions, with two spare wheels, tool kit, spotlight, and stone deflector in front of the grille. Sensible, in its own way, is the lock with which the gearbox—as extensive theft protection—can

be bolted. The wipers, as Daimler-Benz notes fully without irony, come with the car.

The sales remain modest. Only pro forma does the top-of-the-line SS remain in the price list until 1935. In this era of economic crisis, which led at that time to burdensome unemployment statistics of up to almost 20 percent, that is not a very big surprise.

Thus the exclusive nature of the SS actually increases. Of course, no owner needs to bore his neighbors with his car. But whoever wants something really special chooses the bare chassis and has it fitted with an especially exquisite body made by a coachbuilding firm, for example, the Italian specialists, Castagna; the British James & Young; or the Parisian sheet-metal artist, Saoutchik.

For this variant the pleasure starts with the 31,000 Reichsmark that the Mercedes-Benz dealer receives for the delivery of the chassis. The body costs extra—as the buyer chooses. But with that, the chances of winning a trophy for beauty at one of the very popular Concours d'Elegance increase greatly. Ladies wearing hats are inclined to be extremely pleased with such things.

That is pure luxury. And here luxury does not mean comfort, for the super-sport models are not really commodious. Here luxury means the exquisite pleasure of always being able to utilize the most splendid performance, the great charm of being fast, and being in a league that is open only to a small international circle. A market that gives the merchants in Untertuerkheim special pleasure is England. That may sound surprising, because among all-too-conservative thinkers—and they are not only in England—a Mercedes-Benz SS is somewhat unsuitable. They don't run in hill climbs on weekends, but rather have themselves chauffeured to the opera. Instead of a gigantic wooden speedster flinging the SS, with an empty weight of only 1.7 tons, from one curve to the next, they rest in the plushy rear seats.

Whoever drives an SS as a touring and vacation car often goes sailing, plays tennis, and skis. At the end of the twenties and start of the thirties those are very chic sports. But the following sentiment is also involved: "I don't need to develop any blisters on my hands when I drive a car. But I want to."

Technical Data

Make	Mercedes-Benz
Model	Type SS
Years Built	1928–1935
Number Built	~230
Engine Type	in-line six-cylinder, 7,068 cc (431 cu in), 118 to 125 kW (160-170 hp) at 3,200 rpm (with supercharger 147 to 184 kW [200 to 250 hp] at 3,300 rpm)
Gearbox	4-speed
Top Speed	~190 kph (118 mph)
Dimensions	wheelbase 3,400 mm (134 inches)
Weight	~1,700 kg (3,747 lbs)

A real triumphant procession. After Mercedes-Benz's triple victory in the German Grand Prix for sports cars at the Nuerburgring in 1928, they celebrate in Unterrtuerkheim. Caracciola's car is left, Otto Merz's in the middle, and Christian Werner's at right.

The Crown of the Golden Twenties

The Type SSK forms the next step in the direction of motorsport

as of 1928. Its abbreviation still causes enthusiasm today. It ranks

among the unbeaten icons in automotive history.

In the brochure, Mercedes-Benz describes it as "A sports car of class."

The SS proved to be a great seducer. It lured gentlemen drivers and their ladies, offered speed and beauty alike. It won trophies in both racing and *concours d'elegance*. What sounds a bit like an all-purpose weapon now was something completely different: automotive art at the very highest level.

Although it was a derivative, the SS was not a brother in spirit. To be sure, it was very similar technically, but Daimler-Benz applied the focus very differently. While the Type SS could do everything as a supercar, the SSK that came out so shortly after it was the radical type, far more than the already sport-oriented Type S was.

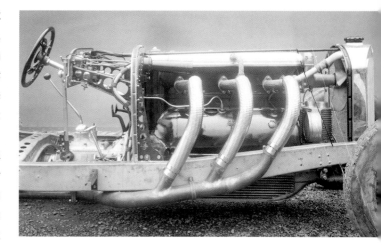

The SSK was more a supercar than a universal car. It had a very hard time making compromises. "With this vehicle we offer the high-class gentleman driver a high-class sporting machine, such as cannot be imagined more completely," said the prospectus somewhat pompously, and proudly listed the performance details: "7.1 liters—6 cylinders—160/200 hp—supercharger—2 special carburetors—dual ignition." The customer could also choose the one of two rear axles that was better suited for his purposes. "If speed records are to be striven for with our SSK model, it is advantageous to deal directly with us about it in the individual case." Thus Daimler-Benz opened further possibilities.

A trunk set comes as a feature on the SSK.

The SSK appeared in 1928, just two weeks after the official premiere of the Type SS on the Nuerburgring which ended with a 1-2-3 victory. The SSK, developed along with the SS, went into the racing car class, with its first start in the hill climb at Gabelbach, Thuringia. Its letters stood for "Super Sport Kurz" because its chassis was 45 centimeters (~18 inches) shorter than that of the SS. For its handling, especially on a hill climb, this reduction was greatly important. The SSK was a superb hill-climb car, a specialist in narrow hairpin curves, just as overwhelming a winner at Schauinsland as at Mont Ventoux, after the competitors from Italy and France threatened to catch up.

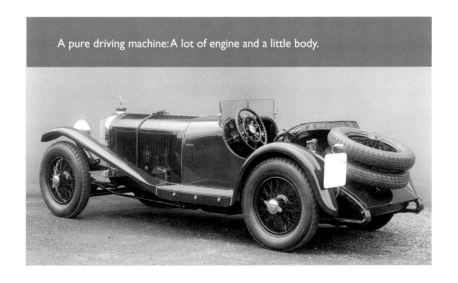

A pure driving machine: A lot of engine and a little body.

Hill climbs like that at Klausenpass became fashionable in the late twenties.

That the new SSK was not lacking in performance was self-evident. It reached back in the series to the strongest engine that the Type SS had: 170/225 HP was standard in the SSK with its 7.1-liter (433 cu in), dual-ignition power plant. If that was not enough for a customer, he could ask at the factory: 250 to 275 hp were doable—for racing, even 300 hp. At the end of the 1920s a competition had arisen in motorsports which cannot be overlooked. Fascinated by the technical and design possibilities, the engineers dared more and more, not only at Daimler-Benz.

At the same time, there were enough sportingly oriented customers who had specific wants. So the Unterturkheimers decided to put out a small series of SSK. In October 1928 it first appeared in Mercedes-Benz's price lists alongside the Type SS. The snappy sportster cost 33,000 Reichsmark, a lot of money. For that sum, Opel delivered almost half a dozen of the "Laubfrosch," the little "auto for everyone." In practice, only a few people

could even afford it, as expensive as the People's Opel was. A Mercedes-Benz was living in its own universe then.

Despite its high performance, it was still "robust and reliable as the best touring car," the catalog promised. And that was in spite of its racing success: "For example, in the German Grand Prix, where, as you know, we finished first, second, and third overall in the last two years, and throughout the difficult races no driver had to open the engine hood."

Because of its shortened chassis, it was no surprise that Daimler-Benz made the body program for the SSK considerably stiffer than with the Type SS. The body works at Sindelfingen delivered a standard two-seat open body of which Daimler-Benz wrote calmly in the prospectus: "This body is purposeful, having two comfortable seats of the highest quality." Now and then a customer also ordered a convertible version.

The SSK (above) or SSKL (below), whether in hill climbs like Koenigsaal-Jilowischt or road races like the Mille Miglia, was a mighty racing sports cars that characterized their era.

With its convincing configuration, the SSK won a resounding reputation in the shortest time. It was the first choice of countless drivers, private as well as professional. Countless races were won by SSK models between 1928, when it made its debut, and the mid-thirties. The SSK is especially interesting because it could run not only in the sports-car but also in the racing-car class. For the latter, the fenders, running boards, top and headlights had to be removed, the SSK racing car was finished. Many a privateer even ran in both classes, one after the other.

With the introduction of the SS and SSK types, an intensive epoch ended at Daimler-Benz in Untertuerkheim. For Ferdinand Porsche, who had come from Austro-Daimler in 1923 with sporting aspirations, left the company. After a short visit to the Steyr works, he became independent in Stuttgart.

In 1931 Daimler-Benz added something again. When the world—and particularly the German Reich—were on the brink of financial ruin, when unemployment and poverty climbed rapidly,

Big, white, and wildly trumpeting, the SSK went into history as "White Elephants."

when production facilities were not kept busy because sales plummeted, even officials had to worry about their pensions. At that time the SSK, farthest removed from practical use, rolled into the dealers' showrooms. Its arrival was an affront that contradicted the developments of the time. And yet, it gave some hope: For one thing, that the world could not yet be lost as long as people and

SSKL a respectable 125 kilograms (275 lbs) of weight. The big boreholes for lightness in the longitudinal members also gave the SSKL something brutal, a reputation that it certainly deserved. Hans Nibel was responsible for the project. After Ferdinand Porsche left, Nibel alone was responsible as the head Daimler-Benz technician. He came from Benz & Cie. in Mannheim, where he was the chief technician since 1908, and had experimented with lightened chassis even there.

The light structure brought a further rise in performance. The plentiful displacement of 7.1 liters was not changed by Hans Nibel, but he raised the compression (now 7.0:1) and installed a bigger supercharger: Enough to give the SSKL 240/300 hp.

Whether the AVUS or the Nuerburgring with its Eifelrennen and Grand Prix, whether the Klausen Pass or other hill climbs, the SSKL won everywhere, and "Rainmaster" Rudi Caracciola was often at the wheel. He was European Mountain Champion for sports cars in 1930 and 1931. Or Hans Stuck, International Alpine Champion in 1932 ("5 starts, 5 wins, and 3 records", the catalog says succinctly)—and, surprise!—Mountain Champion of Brazil. The aerodynamic pioneer Reinhard von Koenig-Fachsenfeld also mounted a streamlined body on an SSKL chassis, somewhat high-sided, and painted red because of the red-ink times, at the beginning of the thirties. The Berlin public, half admiring and half joking, called it "Cucumber" at the German Grand Prix at the AVUS. This special version was some 20

firms think it sensible to invest their time in such things. And for another, because the victories that Mercedes-Benz won in international races made one a little bit proud.

Once again it was Rudolf Caracciola, the hotelier's son from Remagen with Italian ancestors, who secures victories for Mercedes-Benz and Germany. That he, whom they just called "Rudi" or "Carratsch," won the 1931 Mille Miglia in an SSKL was worth far more than just a marginal note. For he was the first non-Italian who could win the wild road race from Brescia to Rome and back, although he could scarcely practice. That was a minor sensation—and took the Italians quite by surprise.

Carratsch's car also won admiration, and was named SSKL a little later—an abbreviation for "Super Sport Kurz Leicht." Light means less here. Countless holes in the chassis, even in the gas and clutch pedals, plus a reworked profile form and deliberate reinforcement here and there, saved the kph (12 mph) faster than the conventionally clad SSKL. It was driven by Manfred von Brauchitsch to a victory at the AVUS in 1932. The spectators noted the speed at 194.4 kph (120 mph)—not at its fastest, but at an average. Otto Merz, the factory driver, crashed fatally a year later with a similar streamlined SSKL. He did not want to wait for rain tires, and he paid for his impatience with his life.

The "legend" concept is severely limited, not only in automobile history. But the SSK, superior as it seemed in its day, earned it. It may be the oldest Mercedes-Benz whose model name was really popular and is still known to insiders today. Although the Mercedes-Benz brand was then so young, it could prove its ability emphatically to all the world with the SSK and SSKL. A famous reputation and great renown are guaranteed, but the SSK scarcely contributed to the economic success of Daimler-Benz. Mercedes-Benz only made about 35 of them by 1933. Only four of the SSKL were built.

The performance of up to 310 hp, which the engineers and engine designer Albert Heess were able to get out of the engine, is particularly attributable to the larger of the superchargers. Its performance was increased again, and it was turned on by hand via a lever under the steering wheel, not by pushing the gas pedal all the way down. The reason for that was the hill climbs, where this blower, built specifically for short-stretch use, had to run constantly.

This piece of technology, being big, endlessly strong, loud, and unshakeable, was simply called the

"elephant" at the factory. And since the impressive SSK and SSKL always came to the start in white, Germany's racing color, they were soon called "white elephants" everywhere. When the SSK started, witnesses noted, their infernal trumpeting really sounded like a herd of elephants. And the supercharger was not yet running—the Roots supercharger made more noise than a dozen circular saws. Yes, it could sound very angry.

Technical Data

Make	Mercedes-Benz
Model	SSK
Years Built	928–1933
Number Built	33
Engine Type	in-line six-cylinder, 7,068 cc (433 cu in), 132 to 177 kW (180-240 hp) at 2,900 rpm (with supercharger 165 to 221 kW [225-300 hp] at 3,300 rpm)
Gearbox	4-speed
Top Speed	190 to 235 kph (118 to 146 mph)
Dimensions	wheelbase 2,950 mm (116 inches)
Weight	~1,700 kg (3,750 lbs) (SSKL: ~1,500 kg [3,305 lbs])

Rarity: This SSK has survived without much restoration. It has a British body.

An Idea Takes Flight

By the end of the 1930s the SSK and SSKL were seen as hard to beat on race tracks and hill climbs. They were also the last models that private owners could buy for use in up to the highest classes of racing. This era finally ended with the Silver Arrows that dominated motorsports from 1934 on.

After World War II everything was different. Including the supercar. The step from the SSK to the 300 SL was a giant step. It seems as if the gull-wing doors had flown over a whole generation.

It is a legend. Even people who do not have cars on their mind, much less old cars, know the gull-wing doors. The 300 SL is a supercar of the highest order—in all aspects. History and ancestry, development and success, rarity and charm are all combined in this vehicle.

It is hard to believe that it can be seen as the direct descendant of the SSK. If the two cars stood side by side, there would seem to be no connection. Actually only about two decades lie between them, a gap that World War II filled with chaos and destruction. With so much prevented development, it is surprising how much has happened between the end of the successful SSK, around 1935, and the first appearance of the 300 SL predecessor. Worlds separate the two concepts; one was born by a massive ladder-frame chassis, the other by a light filigree of tubes. A supercharged 7.0-liter giant drove the SSK; a 3.0-liter with fuel injection powered the 300 SL.

The 300 SL pushed the limits vigorously at the beginning of the 1950s. In 1954 the standard was stepping on the gas pedal in a Beetle out on one of the few Autobahns until the speedometer laboriously climbed over the 100-kph (62 mph) mark. That was all, despite all the noise.

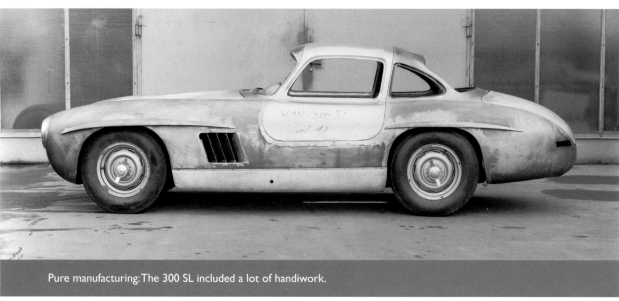

Pure manufacturing: The 300 SL included a lot of handiwork.

The 300 SL looks powerful. At 110 kph (68 mph) the driver has just left second gear. Third gear goes up to 160 kph (~100 mph). Only then does fourth gear take over. Shifting is precise and unspectacular. Down around 4,000 rpm the 300 SL is completely relaxed. Sporting, to be sure, but always poised and eloquent. The mechanics sing softly as you take a fast, well-treated trip in a *Gran Turismo* with its snugly cut but definitely luxurious cockpit. When a 300 SL went by anywhere in the 1950s, mouths gaped open. "I object," an American 300 SL owner complained, "that there are too many people who want to look at the car. I am burdened down with questions."

Its noble restraint, though, leaves the 300 SL when the slim white needle in the chromed circle of the tachometer quickly rises. At this moment the gull-wing discards virtue and morality, forgets all its bonding charm. From 4,500 rpm, now running at 160 kph, it no longer wants to be a dandy. Wildly it storms ahead, becomes loud without losing control over that fortissimo of intake sucking, exhaust barking, and engine howling. It almost seems to rage along the road. Depending on its rear-axle ratio, a 300 SL can reach 250 kph (155 mph). In its day it was the fastest production car in the world.

MERCEDES-BENZ TYP 300 SL

DER „SILBERPFEIL" DES SPORTFAHRERS

Die Erkenntnisse einer weit über ein halbes Jahrhundert reichenden Erfahrung der ältesten Automobilfabrik der Welt im Renn- und Sportwagenbau haben in der Konstruktion des neuen Mercedes-Benz-Seriensportwagens Typ 300 SL ihre Auswertung erfahren. Das rassig-elegante Bild des langgestreckten Wagens läßt schon seine ungewöhnliche Kraft, Schnelligkeit und Wendigkeit empfinden. Seit seinem Erscheinen auf der New Yorker Internationalen Motorschau gehört ihm die Hochachtung der Motorsportfreunde aus aller Welt. Er erweckt die Erinnerung an die ruhmreichen Erfolge der unvergeßlichen „Silberpfeile", der Mercedes-Benz-Rennwagen, und an die von Bern bis Mexico reichende Siegesserie der 3-Ltr.-Sportwagen von 1952, aus denen dieses Fahrzeug entwickelt wurde. Als Repräsentant einzigartiger Tradition und technischer Fortschrittlichkeit bietet der ebenso hochgezüchtete wie betriebssichere Wagen allen Sportwagenfreunden jetzt die Chance, sich bei Wettbewerben und im täglichem Gebrauch die erprobten, ungewöhnlichen Fahreigenschaften des Wagens zu Nutze zu machen, die vorher nur die Werksfahrer des Mercedes-Sterns erlebten.
Der zweisitzige „300 SL" vereinigt die Charakterzüge des Sportfahrzeugs, die extrem hohe Beschleunigung und Geschwindigkeit des Rennwagens und die Annehmlichkeiten eines Tourenwagens. Die aus 215 PS (240 HP aus SAE) erhöhte Leistung des bis zu einer Höchstdrehzahl von ca. 6200 drehzahlfesten Motors mit Benzineinspritzung bietet bei einer Spitzengeschwindigkeit von ca. 260 km/std. seinem Besitzer beste Aussichten in der Klasse „Seriensportwagen" und „Grand Turisme". Gleichzeitig haben ihm seine Konstrukteure betriebliche Unempfindlichkeit, gediegenen Komfort und eine dem ungewöhnlichen Temperament entsprechende Fahrsicherheit verliehen. Dadurch besitzt der „300 SL" alle Eigenschaften eines im Überland- und Stadtverkehr unbedingt zuverlässigen Fahrzeuges.

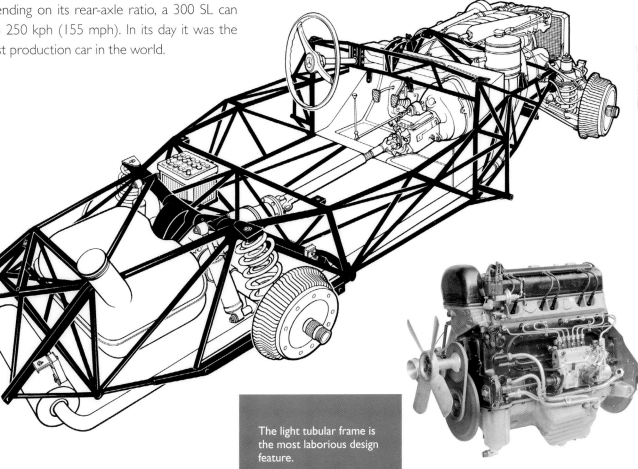

The light tubular frame is the most laborious design feature.

The 300 SL coupe, the sports car of a new generation.

Everything goes on in proper order. Even at high engine speeds, the fuel injection does its duty with Swabian zeal. The Bosch pump supplies all six cylinders precisely with the required amount of mixture in every situation. This technology is brand new; Daimler-Benz developers Hans Scherenberg and Karl-Heinz Goeschel were the first to succeed in making this technique, hitherto tested only in aircraft engines, fit for use in cars. Here the same thing happens as with the supercharger: Despite steadily changing demands, the requirements of an car engine are a good deal more complex than

The folding steering wheel allows husky drivers to get in easily.

No alternative, but a successor: The open 300 SL followed in 1957.

those of an airplane engine. It is fascinating today in retrospect, almost even more than it was then, that this purely mechanical control gives such a precise measurement in all life situations.

The SL marches on. At 5,800 rpm, just under the limit, 215 hp roll off the crankshaft. In the 1950s a troop of seven Volkswagens had to cooperate to produce such power. Dry-sump lubrication provides secure oil supply to the in-line six in all situations. This technology comes from building race cars, like so much of what the 300 SL blends. But not everything is extreme: Its technical basis comes to the sports coupe from the high-class, status-bearing and not at all monstrous Type 300 sedan.

Fun in the snow: Ski star Toni Sailer drives a 300 SL roadster.

The international sports-racing scene loves the fast 300 SL.

The immediate family tree of the 300 SL series goes back to those furious race cars with the W 194 firm code, that collected trophies in the 1952 season: Second and fourth in the Mille Miglia road race, first through third in the Swiss Grand Prix, first and second in the 24 hours of Le Mans, first through fourth in the sports-car race on the Nuerburgring, and a glorious one-two in the exotic and demanding Carrera Panamericana in Mexico. 1952 was a breathtaking year for Mercedes-Benz.

The competitors swallow it when the newspapers write, "Mercedes-Benz builds the world's best sports cars." The star shines again, the return has succeeded after the great pause of World War II. This freshly glowing image calls Max Hoffman onto the scene, an American dealer of Austrian ancestry, who keeps the development departments of German car manufacturers busy as a US importer in the early fifties. He would like these victorious racing cars as production models for the American market. What wild notions! But Daimler-Benz actually reacts. The responsible ones in Untertuerkheim sense that

Spectacular: The 300 SL appears in the Carrera Panamericana and at Le Mans.

the free-wheeling Hoffman is the best key to the highly lucrative market across the Atlantic.

Now the designers work feverishly in Untertuerkheim. They scarcely have the personnel, have only a small budget, their time is short—but they dig into the subject passionately—and have success. At the end of 1952, the first step in the evolution of the original gull-wing door is made. In the works it is disrespectfully called "Plane." In transaxle style with gears on the rear axle, it serves as the test vehicle for another motorsports variant of the 300 SL. The results are exciting, the car is fast, loud, and radical. But then the bosses drop the 300 SL racing project in favor of the Formula I program, with which Mercedes-Benz is active as of 1954.

It's remarkable how fast it all goes. In February 1954 a sensation is waiting on the Mercedes-Benz stand at the New York Motor Show: The new 300 SL—what an exciting coupe! With doors that swing open wide—and that no one ever forgets. Gullwing, they name the new supercar from Germany. It is brand new, unbelievably spectacular, offers a great show. The Americans immediately fall in love with this very cultivated production version of the 300 SL and firmly believe the doors are a styling joke that succeeded. The news rings out that the exotic solution is not a trick, but rather an astounding application of functionalism.

There was already a roadster version of the racing sports car.

crossbars to guarantee sufficient stiffness. A frame bottom layout of pressed sheet steel or even an archaic chassis was refused by Uhlenhaut: With traditional solutions, the 300 SL would have been too heavy and too weak. "A frame should not take on spring powers," Rudolf Uhlenhaut makes clear; that's what springs are there for. A radically simple idea, and simply radical: Aside from two cross members, none of the rigid

If the doors were just for fun, the professional ethics of the integral designers under Chief Engineer Fritz Nallinger would never have allowed such a thing. The "flap doors," as they are called in factory jargon, are simply necessary, so that the occupants can slip through the filigree of tubular-frame design into the inside of the car. Test chief Rudolf Uhlenhaut had created the extremely stiff design of steel tubes for the original SL of 1952—with correspondingly high

Red, black, blue: The colors help the service team recognize the cars quickly.

III. Carrera Panamericana Mexico

Triumphaler Doppelsieg

1. Karl Kling   2. Hermann Lang

Im härtesten 5-Tage-Kampf siegt überlegen in neuer Strecken-Rekordzeit der „Typ 300 SL", entwickelt aus den serienmäßigen Personenwagen von

MERCEDES-BENZ

cannot get into it in graceful elegance. Sporting people, though, to whom the 300 SL appeals, swing themselves calmly behind the wheel in one movement. And for larger drivers, the steering wheel folds down at a joint to create the needed space. That helps somewhat, and is a friendly concession, for in no other detail is the 300 SL nearer to the common people than this.

bicycle tubing is called on to bend. Pushing and pulling are the only forces that work here. The three-dimensional tubular frame weighs only 50 kilograms (110 lbs).

The resulting light structure is a success all along the line. A ready-to-drive 300 SL weighs only 1,310 kilograms (2,888 lbs), thanks to several body parts of aluminum and—as a compromise—the high crossbars. It is not so difficult for a sportsman to get in as is often published. Yes, beyond a certain body size one

A *Gran Turismo par excellence:* the 300 SL is an outstanding fast touring car.

Only 1,400 300 SL coupes were made. About 1,000 of them are thought to exist today.

Exclusive accessories like this set of luggage makes the 300 SL buyer's life sweeter.

How many of the 1,400 buyers of the Gullwing needed this mechanism is not shown in the statistics. What is known is that about 1,000 of the 300 SLs built by 1957 are said to have survived. And the rest? Scrapped at some time? Hardly, at least not intentionally. But there may have been some owners who were carried away by the potency of their cars without having enough talent to control them. It is vital to keep control of this model with the two-joint swing axle at the rear.

This part was already used in the sporting original SL of 1952, when nobody was thinking of series production. Professional drivers got used to the axle that snapped together quite late, but then all the more maliciously. Amateurs less so, and so the handling of the supercar became an issue in its lifetime. Legendary auto tester H. U. Wieselmann, in *auto motor und sport,* specifically warned drivers about the car's all too overwhelming power slides: "The SL can suddenly break loose and

is hard to control in that case." Even capable drivers, he wrote, should "always plan a few percent of play room into theoretical top speed for curves," for safety's sake. For whoever cannot do it flies out faster than he can see—because, as Wieselmann warns, a Gullwing "does not forgive overconfidence." The 300 SL required a relaxed but always-sure hand when it was to be steered quickly through a curve. The able win: This was shown in those years by the countless wins in rallies and long-distance races that the Gullwing took part in worldwide.

The picture of the ever-smart boulevard beau that forms all the same is thus deceiving: Although

prominent people of all colors, heads of state and industrialists order a Gullwing—including the Aga and Aly Khan, shipper Stavros Niarchos. Shah Reza Pahlevi even bought two 300 SLs, and a broad spectrum of German princes and heirs also decided for a 300 SL, as did Alfried Krupp, Herbert von Karajan, the king of Jordan, Tony Curtis, Henri Nannen, and Gunter Sachs. Many of them, and probably all those who never drove one, never suspect that a wild rock 'n roller lurked deep in the 300 SL, and it could beat mightily on the drum. And present-day 300 SL novices should not forget: Everything in it was designed more than half a century ago. Including its drum brakes.

The Americans wanted an open version, so Mercedes-Benz built the second version of the 300 SL as a roadster.

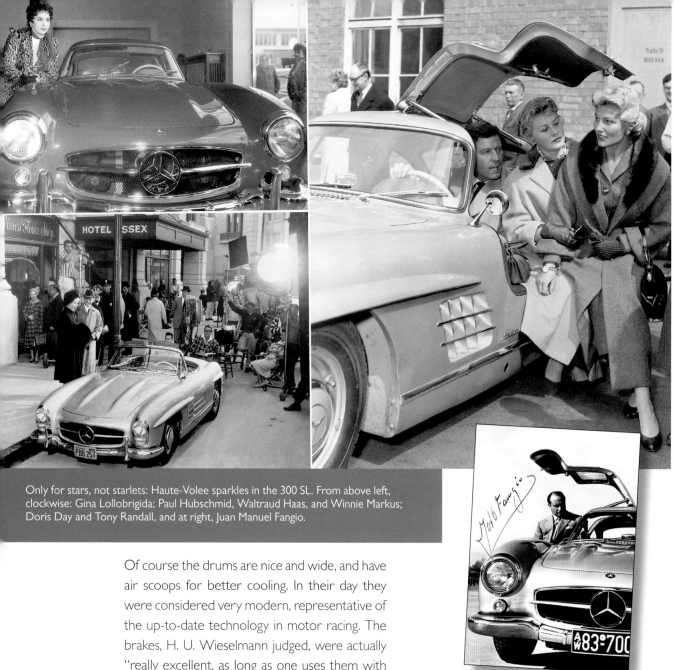

Only for stars, not starlets: Haute-Volee sparkles in the 300 SL. From above left, clockwise: Gina Lollobrigida; Paul Hubschmid, Waltraud Haas, and Winnie Markus; Doris Day and Tony Randall, and at right, Juan Manuel Fangio.

Of course the drums are nice and wide, and have air scoops for better cooling. In their day they were considered very modern, representative of the up-to-date technology in motor racing. The brakes, H. U. Wieselmann judged, were actually "really excellent, as long as one uses them with feeling and understanding. But physical laws must be respected." Yet he asked Daimler-Benz to at

A Striking Shape: The 300 SL is unmistakable.

least think about a two-circuit braking system. The successor to the Gullwing, the 300 SL Roadster, was first fitted with disc brakes in 1961. A two-circuit brake system was introduced in 1963 in the next generation, the 230 SL "Pagoda."

Prettier than the police allow: The Gullwing is still exciting today.

Sculpture for Driving: A 300 SL is more than just an automobile.

In the realm of the supercar, of course, the roadster did not play a major role. Pleasure ranked before sport in it, travel rather than racing was its clear purpose. When the open 300 SL replaced the Gullwing in 1957, this development could be counted as a success by that superb market expert Max Hoffman. He knew exactly that the sun-loving American buyers would rip open cars out of his hands. In Untertuerkheim they bowed to this concept despite the amount of design that rebuilding the tubular frame for an open version would require. In the open version of the 300 SL a single-joint swing axle was also used, taking a little of the fast car's moodiness. By 1963 Daimler-Benz was able to sell 1,858 of the roadster, including, for marketing reasons, two racing sports cars

that had a successful racing season in the United States in 1957 and were also called 300 SLS. In fact, though, the second round of the 300 SL did not sell in great numbers. The worldwide attention and recognition of the brand's name, though, which Mercedes-Benz gained from its top-class sportsmen, has remained incalculable to this day.

It is therefore all the more surprising that Daimler-Benz let the 300 SL run out without a direct successor. The 230 SL, introduced in March 1963, had to replace not only the 190 SL but also the 300 SL, but is conceptually closer to the smaller brother of the 300 SL. On the other hand, the uniqueness of the 300 SL made it become a desired collector's item in the ensuing decades, an icon of automotive history that can raise

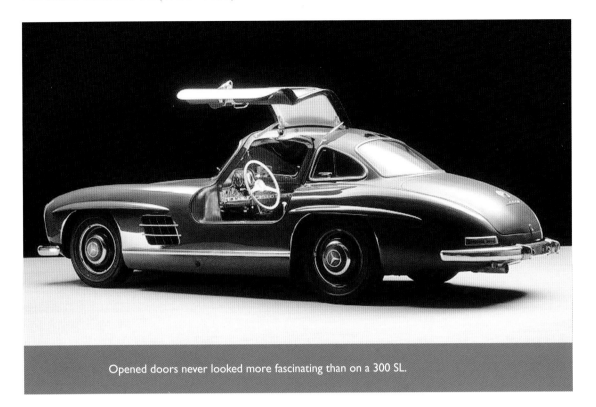

Opened doors never looked more fascinating than on a 300 SL.

Remarkably, the 300 SL remained without a direct successor.

Technical Data

Make	Mercedes-Benz
Model	300 SL
Years Built	1954–1957
Number Built	1,400
Engine Type	in-line six-cylinder, 2,996 cc (182 cu in), 158 kW (215 hp) at 5,800 rpm
Gearbox	4-speed
Top Speed	210 to 260 kph (130 to 162 mph)
Dimensions	wheelbase 2,400 mm (95 inches)
Weight	1,310 kg (2,888 lbs)

tremendous prices on the enthusiasts' market. It is as desired as expensive to this day. The fact that much of its original fascination still lives is not due to its gullwing doors alone, but rather to the harmony of its design. It bears the unmistakable character of its ancestors: "We have made it," said 300 DL developer Rudolf Uhlenhaut, "the way we imagined a sports car."

The Formula 1 Racing Car for the Street

It scarcely gets any more radical: The "Uhlenhaut-Coupe" breaks all the borders of reason. It is not a Gran Turismo, knows no compromises, it wants only to bring radical racing technology to the street.

Does it really belong, the 300 SLR? Is it a supercar—or should it be ranked as a full-blooded racing car?

The 300 SLR is surely a borderline case. It blasts the classic definition of the supercar in several ways. First, because it was never up for sale. It ranks among the so-called blank-check cars: cars for which, after their introduction, solvent collectors and customers immediately sent in checks on which no sum was written. Even that

did not help: Daimler-Benz did not build the cars in series, and the two that were built stayed at the factory.

Point two: The 300 SLR bore a name that sounds deceptively similar to the 300 SL. And at first glance, if one compares the two silhouettes, they show a similarity that cannot be denied. Yet under the well-shaped sheet metal of the 300 SLR there lurks a fully different truth than that of the 300 SL.

Thus the 300 SL, in series production, came close to the everyday definition of the racing sports car of 1952 that was so successful on the track. The 300 SLR, on the other hand, was based on the full-blooded Formula 1 technology that was combined with road-usable bodies. In 1954–55 seven roadsters were created in this manner, and on special request, also two coupes.

The pattern for the development of the SLR technology was set by the new Formula 1 regulations that applied from 1954 on. They called for engines with a maximum of 2.5-liter

Mercedes-Benz engineer Rudolf Uhlenhaut and his baby, the 300 SLR.

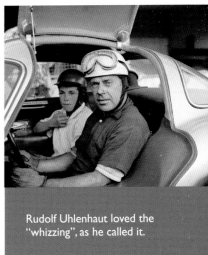

Rudolf Uhlenhaut loved the "whizzing", as he called it.

displacement, or alternatively 750 cc with supercharging. That was somewhat less than before, and besides, at the beginning of the 1950s, Daimler-Benz only had the no- longer-modern Grand Prix engines from the Silver Arrows of the 1930s. Thus a basically new engine arose, a straight-eight divided in the middle for the drive to come off, thus consisting of two blocks with four cylinders each. The desmodromic valves also attracted attention, as did the revolutionary fuel injection that engineer Karlheinz Goeschel distinctively developed.

This engine, tilted 53 degrees in a tubular frame, produced 260 hp at first. The bodies were made of aluminum and magnesium, and were originally formed by hand over shaping blocks. The rear axle was a swing axle, the brakes moved from the wheels to the center to keep the unsprung weight as low as possible. On July 4 the new Formula I racing car started for the first time, and finished first and second in the French Grand Prix in Reims. And at the end of the season, Juan Manuel Fangio was the world champion.

A jump ahead in time: The 300 SLR offers the newest Formula 1 technology.

legendary. With an average of almost 158 kph (98 mph), the two Englishmen raced from Brescia to Rome and back in the 300 SLR. Then, just weeks later, came the dramatic accident at Le Mans, in which more than 80 people lost their lives in June 1955. The management withdrew all the Mercedes-Benz cars from the race.

But after further victories, including the Sicilian Targa Florio, Mercedes Benz was assured of the 1955 World Sports Car Championship. And Mercedes-Benz driver Juan Manuel Fangio won the Formula 1 championship again. In this environment, test leader Rudolf Uhlenhaut had two coupe versions built. The two cars were aesthetically based on the 300 SL series—for example, with their gullwing doors. The difference was the road legality. With a top speed of 290 kph (180 mph), the 310-hp car was for a long time the fastest legal road vehicle. Witnesses declared that it was hellishly loud, especially inside.

But the new technology can be used in other ways, in a wider, more popular class. For 1955 a world championship for sports cars was announced, and Daimler-Benz was interested. The Formula 1 engine grew to 3.0-liter displacement for this use, and the two-seat racing sports car was designated 300 SLR.

Its victory in the Mille Miglia, which Stirling Moss and Denis Jenkinson won in May 1955, was

Gullwing varieties: The fastest was the 300 SLR.

The look deceives: Only from outside does it resemble the 300 SL.

this high-performance car was not banal: "Cold blood, quick reaction, feeling for the machine, and, finally, decisiveness, courage, and endurance" were what the car demanded.

The closed versions of the racing car were to run in long-distance races in the future. Here the 300 SLR coupe was to replace the open version that demanded more of the drivers by speeds that rose from year to year. "I simply wanted to have a closed car for the long-distance races like the Mille Miglia and the 24 Hours of Le Mans, since the drivers are very exposed to the results of differing weather conditions," Rudolf Uhlenhaut explained. "But it would never have been suitable for selling, on account of its very complex technology, with all its reliability in racing." Series production of the 300 SLR was never considered.

This dream ended very soon—at the end of 1955, when Daimler-Benz officially ended its participation in racing. The management had decided on this to save money and spare development capacities. For the Uhlenhaut-Coupe, this end raised many possibilities. Even for the richest collectors or customers the 300 SLR supercar would never have been attainable. Not even in later years: The two examples are still in the Mercedes-Benz collection.

300 hp is frightening in the mid-fifties. The 300 SLR was the world's fastest road car for years.

The two extreme versions quickly became known as the "Uhlenhaut-Coupe." Rudolf Uhlenhaut used one car himself on his daily drive to work and tested it thoroughly—Uhlenhaut loved nothing better than the "whizzing," as he called fast driving. His driving ability was legendary: The engineer was no slower on the track than his best drivers. And he drove home in a controlled drift.

One of the few journalists allowed to test Uhlenhaut's service car thoroughly was Robert Braunschweig, who worked for the Swiss *Automobil Revue*. Even at its top speed of almost 290 kph (180 mph), the coupe ran "absolutely straight, never batting an eye. It was unsensational to excess." And: "Anything less exciting than attaining the top speed was scarcely thinkable." But driving

Under the *Gran Turismo* clothing is pure racing technology.

SSK, 300 SLR: Two worlds, and yet following each other without too many steps in between.

What would have happened if the 300 SLR had gone into series production?

The dream of driving a Formula I car legally in road traffic lived in the 300 SLR.

Technical Data

Make	Mercedes-Benz
Model	300 SLR "Uhlenhaut-Coupe"
Year Built	1955
Number Built	2
Engine Type	in-line six-cylinder, 2,982 cc (~182 cu in), 228 kW (310 hp) at 7,400 rpm
Gearbox	4-speed
Top Speed	~280 kph (~174 mph)
Dimensions	wheelbase 2,370 mm (93 inches)
Weight	988 kg (2,178 lbs)

The Legitimate Heir

In 1969 Mercedes-Benz offered a look into the future: With the C 111 an ambitious test car was created—a true successor to the legendary 300 SL.

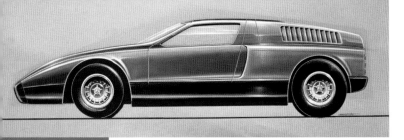

The silhouette leaves no doubt—the engine is in back.

The C 111 proves its good aerodynamics in the wind tunnel.

Now at last the future is beginning. In the autumn of 1969, when the doors to the 44th International Automobile Exposition opened, the breakthrough into a new automotive age finally seemed to begin. The Bosch D-Jetronic, the pioneer of the electronic multipoint injection equipment, had already existed for two years. The first engine management computers were also ready to market, and even functioning anti-lock braking systems were exhibited. They gave a view into what could be possible in tomorrow's cars.

And a car of the future was already in the exposition hall. For days the people crowded toward the Mercedes-Benz. It was the biggest attraction of the 1969 IAA, the C 111, a flounder made of glass-reinforced plastic, with a speed of 270 kph (~168 mph)—and as its greatest surprise, a three-chamber Wankel engine for power. At the end of the 1960s, as again forty years later, they eagerly sought a replacement for the classic piston engine.

The C 111 presented itself as a ready-to-drive test car in which Daimler-Benz had invested several million Marks. Even its color, a metallic golden orange officially called "white autumn," attracted much attention. The excitement gripped auto aficionados from all over the world, collectors, and passionate fans of the brand. They immediately offered blank checks and sent orders to Untertuerkheim. In vain. Even Felix Wankel, who requested a personal test specimen over and over, got nothing. The various versions of the C 111 that would be made would all stay in their makers' possession, and do their work as speedy laboratories carrying a range of devices to test various technologies.

The Wankel is one of them. The rotary-piston concept was a pillar of Mercedes-Benz's research in those years. It could, one hoped, become the engine of the future. The relationship between Daimler-Benz and Felix Wankel's development started eight years before the introduction of the C 111. In the autumn of 1961, Daimler-Benz had bought the rights for the "production of rotary-piston engines producing over 50 hp." That attracted some attention, tension, and great hopes. The C 111 was to fulfill them at the end of the 1960s.

Of course the basic problems with the rotary-piston engine were soon exposed. By 1962 there was already a company-wide crisis meeting to discuss massive problems with moving surfaces and thick sealing strips. There were other firms that took up the rotary-piston technology: NSU went into this market with their Prinz and later Ro 80. Mazda and Citroen also started working on

Mercedes-Benz tries a completely new shape. It is convincing.

Wankel models. So the technology that Daimler-Benz was seeking was no secret. In fact, they were supporting one of the super-trends of the 1960s. Other firms bought all kinds of rights to Wankel engines, including Alfa Romeo, Rolls-Royce, IFA of East Germany, Porsche, Nissan, General Motors, Suzuki, Toyota, and Ford of Cologne. For diesel trucks, MAN, Kloeckner-Humboldt-Deutz, and Krupp obtained production rights. Business was good for Wankel GmbH in the 1960s.

There were many attractive advantages of this new-concept engine. Almost without tangible vibration, the Wankel engines turned fast, like turbines, contained only a few moving parts, and impressed with their very small size. There were also components that had a psychological effect as well, the very challenging allure of being able to write new automotive history in a ground-breaking way with pioneering new technology. It was about nothing less than the new invention of the automobile engine.

It is about nothing less than the new invention of the automobile engine.

The clay models were made by hand.

The C 111 was a pure research vehicle without a commercial background.

The first step of the C 111 began with a three-chamber rotary-piston engine with 600 cc (36 cu in) of chamber volume per chamber. Wolf-Dieter Bensinger, who became the director of engine development for Daimler-Benz after World War I, and had previously worked closely with Felix Wankel, had developed it. Mechanical direct fuel injection took over the fuel mixing, and transistor ignition was used. The engine, at first producing 280 hp, weighed only 150 kilograms (330 lbs); its housing was cast in aluminum. In this form it would take a 3.6-liter conventional engine to equal it.

Now, the Daimler-Benz AG management would have been able to mount test motors in models of current production cars. That happened in part, but in 1968 it was decided to move the subject one notch higher. For one thing, the futuristic Wankel engine would sell much better as a major theme if it was seen in the aura of a supercar—a

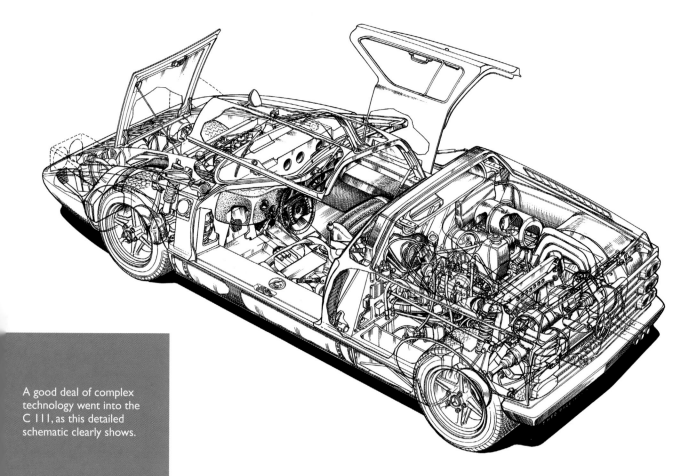

A good deal of complex technology went into the C 111, as this detailed schematic clearly shows.

The C 111 in its 1969 and 1971 variations.

marketing law that is still valid forty years later with electric engines. But secondly, the Mercedes-Benz test department also urgently wanted a mobile test bed for a series of new technologies in the realms of axles and engines, new body materials, and aerodynamic shapes.

The C 111 that project leader Dr. Hans Leibold created offered all of this. At first it was still known as Code 101. Then Mercedes-Benz changed it, first to C 101 and finally to C 111. This last step was not made willingly; Peugeot had obtained the right to the middle zero for car type numbers.

The engineers did not have much time available to develop the new technology carrier. On December 17, 1968, the bosses looked at the first drawings of the new project and nodded. Some of the gentlemen hope that their assent may possibly get them on the way to a timely successor to the 300 SL. The legendary Gullwing and its unbelievable charisma provided hope for the new project.

Compact but powerful: The three-section rotary engine of the C 111.

Rudolf Uhlenhaut was also leading the way in the C 111 project.

The work now goes on in great haste. "We often have not slept for 36 hours," Dr. Hans Liebold later recalled. The C 111 shows the results of those hasty months when it makes its first test runs in April 1969. It is still approaching the goal, and nobody has bothered to consider its aluminum body, which is hammered out in haste. Journalists at first think an evil spirit has been conjured up and see in the crude body the dimensions of a supercar that, hopefully, will soon be ready to market. In the factory they call the first rough body a "plane," as in the woodworking tool.

The C 111 goes into active driving tests.

At the beginning of May 1969 tests were made on the Hockenheim race course, after which the engineers again examined the running gear closely. Several improvements were needed: the rear axle, somewhat irritatingly called the "diagonal swing axle" in factory jargon, came from the still-young W 108. With the dynamics of a C 111, including its wide tires, it was not yet finished, and wretched oversteering made this configuration unusable. A solution of two upper and one lower cross links was tried. It did its job considerably better—and no wonder, it was taken directly from racing experience. In front, refined wheel mounting was developed, the same principle used later in the S-Class introduced in 1972.

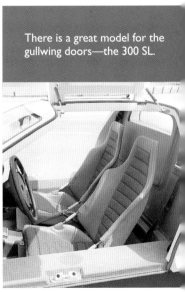

There is a great model for the gullwing doors—the 300 SL.

In the 1970 variant in particular, the shape of the C 111 was convincing from the start.

It was the summer of 1969. While the engineers worked on the technology of the super-sports-car project, the Americans landed on the moon. Technical limits, they thus sowed, are often just imagination. And whoever is clever and ambitious enough can move them.

The experts also worked feverishly on the fiberglass body. It was glued and riveted to a frame that gave it stiffness. Where normal cars have door sills, the C-111 had two safety tanks, and they were so voluminous that conventional doors would not work. Thus the doors swung wide upward, making an impressive picture. Here too, as in the 300 SL, this exalted solution amazingly succeeded in never looking banal.

On July 15, 1969, Rudolf Uhlenhaut, then the car development chief, could examine the first C 111 with a finished body. It was the brilliant engineer's and talented driver's 63rd birthday. "With coffee and cake, the cup in my hand and the cake put off to the side, we drove lap after lap," Theodor Reinhard, body chief of the C 111 project, reported twenty years later to auto journalist Guenter Engelen. "In the car one did not notice the speed. It was like a bus ride."

The public reacts enthusiastically to the supercar.

When the C 111 was at the Frankfurt IAA in September 1969, it gave the fans the ultimate thrill. Beside the still-fresh W 108, the slightly baroque S-Class with its coupes and convertibles, the C 111 looked like a futuristic foundling from another galaxy. Flat, wedge-shaped, potent, and astonishingly balanced in form, the desirable supercar from Stuttgart appeared amazingly different—and yet typical of Mercedes-Benz. Its gullwing doors in particular created a strikingly direct spiritual link with its predecessor.

Between the end of 300 SL production (finally as a roadster) and the first appearance of the C 111, no more than six years had passed. Yet if one sees the two standing side by side, several generations of models seem to belong between them. And they handle so differently, too. Despite how modern the C 111 is, the driver still has to use lots of gas and engine speed. Below about 5,000 rpm, the Wankel is subdued instead of joyful.

Five of the first C III series were built. There was no time for more, for behind the curtains, the team around Hans Liebold and engine chief Wolf-Dieter Bensinger developed, in only about six months, the C III that made its debut at the Geneva Salon in March 1970. It can do everything a good bit better. Now thanks to the building-block system, the Wankel quickly grew to four chambers producing over 350 hp at 7,000 rpm. That equals no less than a good 4.8 liters of conventional displacement—with a weight that has grown by 20% but, at 180 kilograms (397 lbs), is still sensationally low. The definitely cultivated engine offers a third more torque from considerably lower engine speeds, and the top speed rose to beyond the 300 kph (185 mph) region. In just 4.9 seconds the C III sprinted from zero to 100 kph (62 mph).

The most astounding aspect is that the mid-engine sports car was very unproblematic. Even Formula I drivers of the time who were allowed to drive a C III were excited about the smoothness of the car, even in the borderline area. "An unexcelled combination of comfort and roadholding" is offered by the C III, said legendary auto tester Paul Frere in 1970 in *auto motor und sport* after a test drive.

The body, also reworked in many details, also contributed. Aerodynamics is an important aspects of it, as proved by the cW value lowered by 8% and the drive to the front wheels, improved by 20%. In fact, the designers even took comments on the miserable all-around view from the original C III version into consideration when they reworked the design. Now even this criticism is outdated, and the interior is so obviously improved that it can already be regarded as ready for series production. Even a radio was installed, and for the traveling luggage of the C III passengers, Mercedes-Benz showed a set of three magnificent suitcases at the 1970 Geneva Salon.

The two variants of the C 111 in front of the first test vehicle.

"The car is of such perfection that one believes the first customer would stand at the Untertuerkheim gates tomorrow to pick up this car," wrote auto journalist and Mercedes-Benz expert Guenter Engelen in 1989. It is no wonder that more and more interested parties came knocking on Daimler-Benz's door. Even the Shah of Iran was there. They insist on a small series—and make no impression. Tester Paul Frere also wished in *auto motor und sport* in 1970 that the C 111 would "go into production as an ultra-fast GT car. It would be not only the most comfortable and quietest, but at about 300 kph (186 mph) also the fastest such car."

The increased performance and further developmental success of the C 111, with all its technical concepts, have not brought much luck. Even its prominent, active defenders, notably CEO Dr. Joachim Zahn, Dr. Hans Scherenberg, and Rudolf Uhlenhaut, have had to admit slowly that they probably drove into a dead end with the Wankel. Others, though, have predicted from the start that the project would surely fail. The responsible parties at Mercedes-Benz have not stood in unity behind the Wankel experiment. This experiment was too daring, too expensive, the technology was too untameable. In short, a wrong way. Only for a moment, rumor has it, have the bosses seriously considered the idea of a small series, which then would have had a conventional engine. But in the end, the courage to say "yes" has been lacking.

The end of the Wankel engine: A successful 64-hour record run with the C-III, now driven by a diesel engine, on the Nardo test track in Italy in 1976.

The final nail in the coffin for the once hopeful C III with its Wankel engine came in 1973. Its lavish consumption cannot be halted, and the trend toward stricter exhaust regulation—especially in California—caused problems for the Wankel. There were difficulties with ignition, to say nothing of the problem of meager long-term running characteristics. The available seals were not trusted to get by over long running times with much reliability. Yet Daimler-Benz still places special emphasis on reliability, a basic virtue of the brand.

But the experiments went on. A little later a C III even ran with an automatic transmission. A two-stage injection system was also put to use. In the end, of course, only a good 300 hp remained, but the powerful pull, thanks to the torque and present in all situations, is inspiring.

Then, in 1976 the second C III was given a new task. Instead of continuing with the Wankel, it was now supposed to do the same with the new five-cylinder turbo-diesel engine. Fast diesels? Unthinkable at the time. In the mid-1970s, dynamic oil-burners were thought to be as utopian as mobile phones. As C III-IID, it set out on the high-speed oval at Nardo, in southern Italy, and broke all international speed records for diesels. And not just those.

Instead of the 80 hp that the engine in the Series 123 300 D achieved, the 3.0-liter diesel, tuned by all the rules of the art and also turbocharged, now achieved an unbelievable 190 hp. In Nardo it covered a stretch of 10,000 kilometers (6,213 miles) at an average speed of more than 252 kph (~157 mph). And it remained true to the typical qualities of the Mercedes-Benz diesel: It is reliable, long-lived, and thrifty. As a new attribute, it can quickly be added that this combination made an impression all over the world. It is unbelievable what the folks in Stuttgart squeezed out of a diesel.

to 230 hp by an additional blower air filter and countless other measures. Nardo again, a world record again: in 1978 the third C 111 generation sets nine new marks. This diesel went almost 330 kph (205 mph). In the process it produced news that drew much applause: Even at a sustained speed of more than 300 kph (186 mph), its consumption was only 16 liters per 100 kilometers (15 miles per gallon).

Finally, there comes the last stage of this small, experimental, and record-setting C 111 series. Nobody has spoken of possible series production in ages; no wonder, as the body looks more and more like an airplane's fuselage with twin tailfins in back and concealed wheels. The C 111-IV, with a classic V-8 engine from a 450 SE (W 116) won the crown for the C 111 models: The bored-out 4.8-liter engine produced reliable 500 biturbo horsepower at 6,200 rpm. It pushed the car, meanwhile aerodynamically very refined, ahead impressively.

And sure enough, Nardo again, a record again: At almost 404 kph (250 mph) it beat its former best mark for the fastest round-track speed by more than 48 kph (30 mph)—until then, a Porsche 917/30 had held that record, a mighty car that produced more than 1,000 hp, twice that of the C 111. But a power deficit? The Mercedes-Benz, with its excellent aerodynamics, smoothed that out. This result especially pleased Hans Liebold, the project leader of the experimental series, who also drove the C 111-IV during the record runs.

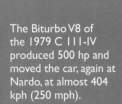

World records could also be celebrated in 1978: The C 111-III, with its 230-hp, five-cylinder turbo-diesel reached a top speed of almost 330 kph (205 mph).

They even expanded the diesel experiment. Only two years later, a clearly overworked C 111 rolled into public view, no longer street-suitable in its new bodywork, but as a pure record car. Only the bottom of it came from the earlier C 111 models, with the wheelbase lengthened by 110 millimeters (4.25 inches), the track reduced to 150 and 100 mm (6 and 4 inches). Whoever saw this C 111 immediately recognized the break with the former C 111. Longer, more radical, flatter, the diesel record car appeared, painted silver in the tradition of earlier racing and record cars.

This evolutionary step of the C 111 also used a five-cylinder turbo-diesel, its power increased

The Biturbo V8 of the 1979 C 111-IV produced 500 hp and moved the car, again at Nardo, at almost 404 kph (250 mph).

Ultimately, it was not its unattainability that made the C 111 one of the most desirable of all automobiles. And presumably there is no other model that has remained as renowned over the decades as the C 111, although it was neither sold nor employed in motorsports. It is the pop-star among the technology carriers—and would so gladly have become a supercar in a small series.

An orange like no other; it became the symbol of the C 111.

The high-speed run was certainly more than just proving Daimler-Benz can go in a circle faster than others. The engineers gained countless knowledge of the performance of material and aerodynamics at extreme speeds from the fast laps at Nardo. It remained a marginal note that the actual record was not recognizable in principle for matters of form. That was already known in advance, but this statement is strong enough even outside regulations.

Hans Liebold's C 111 models went down in history as prototypes of a sports-car generation that, despite the best stuff, did not make the jump into series production. Five examples of the first series and six of the second were built. Three cars of the first series were scrapped by Daimler-Benz, and in January 1970 one car was totaled during test drives at Hockenheim. But nine C 111s have lived on in the factory collection.

Technical Data

Make	Mercedes-Benz
Model	C 111
Year built	1970
Number Built	6
Engine Type	four-rotor rotary engine, 4 × 600 cc (36 cu in) chamber volumes, 268 kW (365 hp) at 7,000 rpm
Gearbox	5-speed
Top Speed	300 kph (186 mph)
Dimensions	wheelbase 2,620 mm (103 inches)
Weight	1,287 kg (2,837 lbs)

Very Close to Life

The plans were great. Producing the C 112 would have opened a new class of cars to Mercedes-Benz. But nothing came of this idea—it remained a single car for research purposes.

ts name says everything: C 112. It follows right after C 111, that technology carrier introduced in 1969 that tried to do everything, at least to get into automotive history as a small series. It had the goods to do it.

Twenty-two years lay between the debut of the C 111 and the first appearance of the C 112. In September 1991 it was introduced at the Frankfurt IAA as the new technology carrier. Months before that, there was already discussion and speculation—as with the C 111. And as with that, the fans' dreams remained unfulfilled in the end. There would never be series production.

The C 112, as Mercedes-Benz saw it, was to determine the border between active and passive safety. With it, the effects and dependencies of various components were to be tested thoroughly. At the same time, it offered a look at the technical potential that supercars of the 1990s would have. That much of it, though not all, had to be new, was seen by the first glance at its doors. They swung upward, hinged at the roof—just as they did in 1952 in the first racing sport version of the 300 SL. The C 111 picked up that motif in 1969; the C 112 followed in 1991: Doors opening to the skies were part of the family heritage. As a symbol, they unite these supercars with Mercedes-Benz's star logo.

At its premiere, the flat C 112 was often and happily compared with the Sauber-Mercedes C 11. That sports prototype reached 400 kph (~250 mph) with its five-liter, V-8 mid-engine. It was successful too: In the 1990 season the Sauber-Mercedes C 11 won eight of nine races, its team won the world

The lines mirror the accepted styling of the 1990s.

championship—a towering achievement. The direct predecessor of the C 11 was the Sauber-Mercedes C 9, which scored a 1-2 victory in the 1989, 24-hour Le Mans with, among others, Jochen Mass driving.

At first glance, to be sure, the C 112 supercar study scarcely depended on its motorsport relatives. Only the form of the roof cupola indicated distant similarity. Yet the C 112 bore many genes that came directly from auto racing. In the chassis, for example, the monocoque tub of bonded aluminum and plastic completes an aluminum tube frame that gave the light body of the C 112 more rigidity and also served as a roll cage.

The low door sills catch the eye.

The winged door theme remained fascinating.

From the start, the C 112 was usable on the road.

On the other hand, as a supercar, it stood in the midst of life. From the start, it was usable on the road, a model that had to fulfill all the requirements. That fundamentally differentiated it from one of those car studies that are mainly playgrounds for stylistic ambitions. With the C 112, the strange possibility would be offered of "creating an absolute automobile in which no red line might be drawn on the expense of technology," as *auto motor und sport* wrote in 1991. The C 112 was supposed to "show what we can do," said the then head of the passenger-car division, Juergen Hubbert.

Looking back, it also seems interesting that performance and speed were no longer the undisputed heart of a supercar, as had been confidently taken for granted in earlier years. Along with its glorious Le Mans-winning history, which was mentioned in passing, the C 112 was now about safety, comfort, and environment.

To avoid treating the theme of propulsion too casually, Mercedes-Benz chose the production V-12 engine from the S-Class 600 E "battleship" of the new W 140 series. It was the strongest available induction engine and produced 408 hp. As a mid-engine, it found its new home ahead of the rear axle of the C 112. A six-speed gearbox, as soon as it was completely developed, was to pass on the plentiful power. Expected things like ABS, anti-slip regulation, automatic climate control, and a lavish sound system were all on board.

There was also plenty of new technology. For example, a variable brake-power distribution, the brand new Active Body Control (ABC) running-gear correction, and self-regulating cybernetic rear-axle control, which constantly corrected course aberrations from ruts, side winds, or different types of road surfaces. All in all, these measures were especially effective.

The electronic-hydraulic ABC was based on earlier steel springs, in which every leaf was completed by a hydraulic cylinder working in one direction. Via a rod and rocker, this individually regulated the pressure on the spring. With that, the ABC could even out all nodding and rolling movements that occurred, particularly in curves, on braking, or acceleration. Classic stabilizing, though, could be eliminated in this system, but not shock absorbers. They still served to dampen very frequent oscillations. The system hydraulics could, of course, change the recognition lines of the shock absorbers.

So that the system functioned, countless sensors had to send their initial data to a control device. This calculated the necessary corrective means in real time and sent appropriate impulses to the controllable elements. The ABC was years ahead of its time. It would not be until 1999 that this system could be installed in a production car.

A fascinating idea: plenty of intermediate positions.

S - C 112

How important the integration of futuristic solutions was to Mercedes-Benz in the C 112 is shown by the fact that a small disadvantage of this system was knowingly taken in the bargain: It added some 25 kilograms (55 lbs) to the car's weight. Calculations originally gave the car an empty weight of about 1,200 kg (2,645 lbs). But the wealth of technology leaves its mark. When the C 122 finally appeared at the IAA, it weighed about 1,600 kg (3,527 lbs).

The body shape was originated at Sindelfingen. It was elegant in an engineering sense, rather restrained and undoubted. Optimal aerodynamics took the focal position for the body experts. The developers spent a long time in the wind tunnel. It was not simple to unite opposites optimally. Finally, an optimally wind-sucking shape opposed the wish for high deflection. For example, this was proved by Formula 1 cars whose cW value is often remarkably high. With an air-resistance value of 0.33, the Mercedes-Benz body developers finally found a good compromise between deflection and induction for the C 112.

The fact that it succeeded so well without the theatrical device of adding a rear spoiler is also due to the active aerodynamics of the C 112. In tenths of a second, setting engines correct the horizontal flat spoiler at the front and the rear wing, which could be set high or at an angle as needed. Thus along with the suspension and brake changes, these changing aerodynamics particularly helped the car to remain stable on the road in critical driving situations. The C 112, although technically limited to a top speed of 250 kph (155 mph), could always reach about 310 kph (~193 mph) without problems.

On curves or when braking, the pressure, especially on the rear axle, could suddenly be increased greatly, to the point at which the steeply elevated rear panel became a real air brake. This idea had its first experimental use some forty years before in the pre-series phase of the 300 SL. It would, though only 13 years after the C 112, finally go into production in the Mercedes-Benz SLR McLaren.

The C 112 took advice from auto racing.

An air brake completed the job.

In the C 112 the active aerodynamics and the brake pressure distribution were coupled. Depending on the power of the deflection, a control device sent more power to the brakes on the rear axle. The more air pressure, the stronger the braking.

Active driving safety was a central theme of the C 112. A radar gap-distance warning helped to avoid driving accidents, and the C 112 even had a tire-pressure monitor. But it was also strong in the realm of passive safety. Its own catching mechanism held the engine away from the passengers in case of a crash. This also protected the roll bar in the passenger space. If a C 112 was left lying upside down after an accident, the passengers, despite the wing doors, had a good chance of leaving the car quickly. A sensor-controlled hinged panel above the door windows, even in such a precarious situation, allowed them to climb out of the overturned C 112. Quick help from outside was also possible.

The C 112 could have become the new 300 SL.

The C 112 had an integral wing at the rear.

121

Useful every day: Under the sheet metal was the V-12 engine of the S-Class.

Mercedes-Benz did everything to overcome the problem of road eligibility for the C 112. For that reason, the hot 750-hp, biturbo V-8 of the Le Mans winner was not used in the C 112, but rather that spirited but gentle V-12 of the new S-Class. But inside as well, the C 112 proved to be comfortable and homey. "As a contrast to the classic metallic gray of the outer skin, inside

there are blue tones of all kinds, nicely decorated with red stripes, along with a few relaxing black surfaces," as Bernd Ostmann wrote in *auto motor und sport* in 1991.

The package is alluring, and so it is not surprising that some 700 collectors and fans from around the world seriously inquired about its possible availability. Even the rumors that the sales price would be above the million-Mark border did not stop them from sending blank checks to Daimler-Benz. But their signals were unsuccessful; the management decided not to build the C 112 in series. In June 1992 *auto motor und sport* reported that the checks were sent back to the pleading customers in March of that year with thanks for their confidence. But the firm was not in a position "to fulfill the wish for the Mercedes-Benz C 112 supercar in the foreseeable future."

Maybe it was the fear of their own courage? In *auto motor und sport,* auto journalist Clauspeter Becker cited the critical basic mood of the early 1990s—cars like the C 112 scarcely had a chance. "And the course of time works against a sports car with 300 kW of power, 300 kph [186 mph] top speed, and a price of a million Marks or more."

"No one for all," *auto motor und sport* said dejectedly in August, and yet portrayed the car thoroughly. As the IAA came nearer, a few people had not completely lost hope for series production. In the end, the idea to find an heir, at last, that would not be completely lost in the great footsteps of the blessed 300 SL seemed more than attractive. It was said Mercedes-Benz had even found a coachbuilder for a possible small series—the Cucciola firm of Turin, where the aluminum prototype was made.

The exotic doors, in any case, would not have been a problem. During the designing phase, Daimler-Benz concretely found out from the proper authorities whether a production car with gullwing doors could be authorized for road use. Since 1960 that had only been possible with special permission. It would have worked.

But then everything came out different. After the 1991 IAA, Daimler-Benz hastily drew a line

Technical Data

Make	Mercedes-Benz
Model	C 112
Year built	1991
Number Built	1
Engine Type	V-12, 5,987 cc (365 cu in), 300 kW (408 hp) at 5,200 rpm
Gearbox	6-speed
Top Speed	~250 kph (155 mph)
Dimensions	unknown
Weight	~1,600 kg (3,527 lbs)

under the project. The star of the show rolled away from the public eye, not even to experience its road testing. It seems the time was not yet right for such a car. Not yet.

The C 112 remained an individual.

Super-Flat, Super-Expensive, Super-Rare

It took a generation before Mercedes-Benz again offered a supercar for sale. But then only thirty of them were made. The CLK-GTR remains one of the most exclusive Mercedes-Benz's driving experiences. One of the fastest, anyway.

It looks like a CLK but could not be more dissimilar.

Even the most loyal fans do not have that much time: Mercedes-Benz waited for 43 years. Four long decades without introducing a new supercar that people could buy. Yes, they proudly exhibited the C 111 and C 112, the Untertuerkheimers did not deliver one for a buyer's garage for either money or good words. A long drought prevailed, through which the sporting faction among the enthusiasts suffered. And that was in a pause in which the world experienced a string of fascinating supercars, from the Porsche 911 to the BMW M1 and the Lamborghini Countach. Just no more of those that bore the Mercedes star. The last one had been the legendary gullwing 300 SL in 1954.

But then in April 1997 the bomb went off:

The CLK-GTR was coming! In the old tradition, Mercedes-Benz wrote very modestly and factually to the journalists: "CLK-GTR is a new high-performance sports car by Mercedes-Benz that is the basis for participation in the GT championship of the international automobile organization FIA." Or, no less wooden, "Super-coupe as the highest level of the new CLK." Those are definitely dry words to the press about a powerful automobile.

For the CLK-GTR really had the right stuff. It lurked on the road, extremely flat, and one could say, if one were restrained, that beauty is relative. It looked a bit as if it were one of the new CLK models that got stuck under a gigantic steamroller.

An extreme look at the CLK-GTR on a road trip.

Everyone recognizes it at once: That is a Mercedes CLK.

The result: from the 137-cm (54-inch) height of the original CLK, only 116 cm (46 inches) remain. The two models have only their name in common—and a few design quotations: By the grille, the headlights, and the window silhouettes of the extreme coupe, the readers of the 1997 *Auto Magazine* recognize the CLK again at once. It forms, as Mercedes-Benz defines it, the "formal basis" of the new supercar. But the bonus is that the CLK-GTR is really allowed to drive on public roads and—three cheers!—is actually to be produced in small numbers.

While the appearance was still based somewhat on the CLK, that cannot be said of the technology. It was, as Mercedes-Benz again states, coolly formulated: "An individual development with the most modern top-class technology".

Thus not only the body, but also the monocoque of the CLT-GTR under it, was made of carbon fiber, the still-new and sinfully expensive material for car building in the 1990s. The bearing structure weighed only 80 kilograms (176 lbs). And where the monocoque ended at the rear, at the wall right

The big V-12 engine from the S-Class powers it.

behind the two seats, there was a voluminous four-valve, V-12 engine installed, which originally made its home in the S 600 luxury limousine of the W 140 series. It became a mid-engine here, and it produces. Enlarged to 6.9 liters for this car, it produces 612 to 631 hp, depending on the version, and offers 720 Nm—clearly more of everything than the six-liter, 394 hp, and 570 Nm of the limousine. A "race-tested," straight-toothed, six-speed gearbox with sequential shifting transfers the power to the rear wheels. The GTR had it all, and everything was newly developed: Air intake, springed exhaust elbows, exhaust system including catalytic converter, engine angled to the left, a crankshaft that supplied 7.8 mm (0.3 inch) more stroke, different pistons, rods and camshafts, different valve drive, injection system, and cylinder heads.

Remarkably, much of the basic layout of the CLK-GTR is reminiscent of the C 112 research car that appeared six years before. That applied, for example, to the bearing structure of a monocoque with attached mid-engine, which came as a V-12 from the S-Class W 140. Even a sequential six-speed gearshift appeared earlier on the C 112.

In the autumn of 1997 the CLK-GTR is shown at the Frankfurt IAA. There is a slight gasp from the fans. Even though there are not many who can really be happy: Only 25 examples of the CLK-GTR are to be built by AMG, the tuning and racing specialist firm partnering with Mercedes-Benz. At least one is registered with the FIA for participation in the GT championship. It is less well-known that the FIA also defined a price limit of a million US dollars. That was a lot of money

Not gullwing doors, but still a spectacular solution.

in 1997, but no problem for collectors, of whom there were enough—for Daimler-Benz had already received many blank checks for even the non-marketed C 111 and C 112. And the same was true for the legendary 300 SLR of 1955—that model called the "Uhlenhaut-Coupe" that was nothing more than a Formula 1 disguised by a body reminiscent of the Gullwing 300 SL. That 300 SLR was one of the ancestors of the CLK-

GTR, surely the most legitimate one: It already offered pure racing technology in road-accepted trim. On the other hand, the C 111 and C 112 seemed somewhat more academic. As fascinating as they were, their purpose as study and research vehicles always limited the same unlimited racing joy that the 300 SLR truly contained in every bit of its design.

Extreme roadster: There is also an open CLK-GTR.

The fresh-air variant was limited to five examples.

As for the CLK-GTR, it was certain, many a fan would reach for it at any price in 1997. AMG is said to have received 200 definite orders—before the price was even announced. Whoever was lucky enough to be chosen had to send the paltry sum of 3,074,000 Marks to Mercedes-Benz. And have patience. For in favor of the Stuttgart folks, the FIA changed the rules so that participation in the championship was already possible, although the cars needed for homologation were not yet built. When the time came in 1998, the racing CLK-GTR had long since won the 1997 and 1998 world championships convincingly—against competition that included, among others, Porsche, Lotus, and BMW-McLaren. In the 1997 season, Bernd Schneider also won the driver's championship. The CLK-GTR won six of eleven races, with four 1-2 victories and four other second places in the chronicles.

As spectacular as the gullwing doors once were, the CLK-GTR doors were equally spectacular.

Everything is a little different: The front and back can be removed completely with just a few moves.

The 25 completed CLK-GTRs showed in an exciting way the split that Mercedes-Benz and AMG had risked to win the GT championship on the one hand, and, on the other, to offer an ultimate yet typical Mercedes-Benz driving experience on the road. Safety also played an essential role in its development.

Mercedes-Benz dominated the FIA GT class with the CLK-GTR.

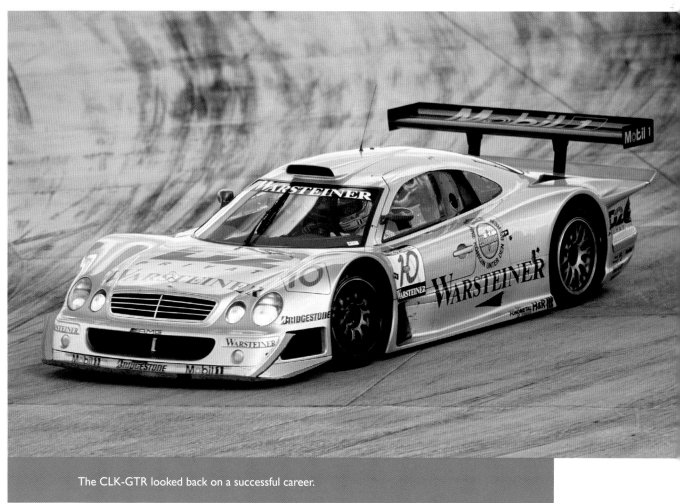

The CLK-GTR looked back on a successful career.

133

Whoever can, makes an Alpine tour in a CLK-GTR roadster.

Driving the CLK-GTR was a tremendous experience.

Thus besides the roll bar integrated in the carbon-fiber monocoque, there was the crash box prescribed in racing. In the street version of the CLK-GTR there were air bags for the driver and passenger on board, plus the restraint system from the CLK, which worked with its belt tighteners and belt power-limiters. ABS and ASR were likewise self-evident, as were several creature comforts like full glass windows, a standard audio system with CD changer, remote control locking, and air conditioning. All of that, of course, made the weight increase from the 1,000 kg (~2,205 lbs) of the racing version to 1,400 kg (3,086 lbs) for the road version. Malte Juergens wrote in *auto motor und sport* that "compared to the racing version, the

fine body finish, filling materials, and extensive paint layers added another 50 kilograms [110 lbs]" to the CLK-GTR. Customers even received their own set of luggage with the CLK-GTR.

The vehicle's whole architecture followed the basics of auto racing. The engine, attached to the monocoque and also to the gearbox, took on a load-bearing function. In back, the wheel suspension connected directly with the gearbox. As in front, there were double transverse links, gas-pressure shock absorbers and manually adjustable stabilizers. The pierced brake discs were made of cast gray metal; the carbon version was reserved for the thoroughbred racing versions of the CLK-GTR. At 380 (front) and 355 (rear) millimeters (~15 and 14 inches), they are generously dimensioned, and along with four- and six-piston floating calipers of aluminum, they assured the best slowing even in hard use. The external tire formats—front 295/35 ZR 18, rear 345/35 ZR 18—gave rise to much admiration in 1997. Such sizes were then anything but common on road vehicles.

It is no surprise that the CLK-GTR was fast. With a top speed of 320 kph (~200 mph) and 0-to-200-kph (124 mph) acceleration in only 9.9 seconds (0-100 kph [0-62 mph] in 3.7 seconds), one could assume that there was enough performance at hand. Is it a surprise that it was not enough for some owners? At least two, and some sources speak of three other CLK-GTR owners ordered larger, stronger engines from AMG. Thanks to 7.3 liters of displacement, the performance increased to 664 hp, and possibly even 10% more.

Driving the CLK-GTR was a remarkable experience. Even larger drivers could get into the cockpit fairly easily, thanks to doors that swung upward and a removable steering wheel—both features reminiscent of the iconic 300 SL. And here again there was a high door sill, almost half a meter wide, to get over before reaching the interior. Despite the leather-upholstered comfort, the occasional driver hoped in vain for electric seat adjustment. For buyers of the CLK-GTR, though, that was not a problem. They received their seats made to measure.

"The engine turns like lightning and amazingly high," Malte Juergens noted. "The driving experience is of that intensity that makes lovers of excess sigh with pleasure." The CLK-GTR did not race, as one would call it, but shifting up into third gear was "like three mighty leaps from rpm limit to rpm limit." Bernd Ostmann was also excited. The editor-in-chief of *auto motorsport* called the CLK-GTR a "real straight-line gobbler," that springs "over short distances like a skipping-stone on the water."

The steering and handling also convinced the testers. "Precise, unbelievably agile, and very sensitive, the heavy coupe follows the sensitively responding servo steering," said Juergens. "It sneaks through bends of all radii and brakes as if the tires had taken a bath in quick glue before the turns." Bernd Ostmann added that the CLK-GTR "springs right into the turns. The servo steering is finely adjusted for it, not too insensitive, but going lightly enough."

And although the CLK-GTR was obviously a racing car, the "typical Mercedes character unmistakably" remained in effect, said Mercedes-Benz factory driver Bernd Schneider. Malte Juergens tried to express it more philosophically: "On the race course the CLK-GTR embodies the pure theory of power and good feeling like scarcely any other car." In any case, the fact is that the big 12-cylinder engine of the CLK-GTR, with its large volume, won respect. The keening, high-pitched whine of nervous racing engines was foreign to it.

From the end of 1998 to the summer of 1999, Mercedes-Benz had the CLK-GTR built in a small series of 25 cars. It is amazing how fast the motorsport specialists of AMG in Affalterbach finished their developmental work; between the contract from the management and the finishing of the first CLK-GTR, no more than 128 days passed. After two weeks the new engine was already running. That left its mark: "In the last month we slept as much as normally in a week," a happy but exhausted AMG mechanic reported to *auto motorsport* journalist Guido Stalm.

Five very special examples of the CLK-GTR were turned out in 2002 by AMG. They had no roof and were thus the exotics among the exotics.

Glutted with performance and uncommonly agile despite the high weight: the CLK-GTR roadster.

In this extreme roadster, the genes of pure racing technology unite with hedonistic open-driving joy to form a spicy mixture. It makes little sense but much fun.

And that should not go away for a long time, of course the gearboxes and clutches, taken straight from racing cars, were not made for equal measures of durability as the components of a production CLK. The powerful V-12 engines, on the other hand, have no weaknesses; Juergen Mattheis, H.W.W. manager, is sure of that. In 2003 he asserted to *auto motorsport:* "Nothing gets broken there. It runs easily over 100,000 kilometers (62,137 miles)." For supercars of this kind, that is a rather surprising statement.

Bernd Schneider had come right to the point: The car has a typical Mercedes character.

Technical Data

Make	Mercedes-Benz
Model	CLK-GTR
Year built	1997
Number Built	25 + 5 (2002)
Engine Type	V-12, 6,898 cc (420 cu in), 457 kW (621 hp) at 6,800 rpm
Gearbox	6-speed
Dimensions	wheelbase 2,670 mm (105 inches)
Weight	1,440 kg (~3,175 lbs)

Mercedes-Benz Starts in a New League

As opposed to its namesake, this new SLR is regularly on the price lists. With it, Mercedes-Benz finally offers a thoroughbred supercar again. The SLR McLaren successfully plays up front in the major league.

Luxury also counts:
The SLR McLaren
makes no sacrifices.

"Never yet," the readers of *sport auto* learned in 2004, was it "so simple to venture so far into hitherto unknown territory with 626 hp." Horst von Saurma, sports-car tester by profession, knows exactly what he's talking about. The SLR McLaren, on the one hand, fascinates with a brachial but safely tamed power, and at the same time offers a fundamental utility, such as every Mercedes driver expects from his/her car.

It cannot be cataloged simply, this supercar with the name of SLR McLaren, which Mercedes-Benz marketed as of 2004. On the one hand it wants to be a supercar. On the other, it has classic *Gran Turismo* heredity. Perhaps it is "just a perfect mixture of the two?" asks *sport auto* in the framework of the "supertest." That could be it. But nobody may expect simple answers from an extreme car, as the SLR McLaren is anything but simple.

The responsible parties at Mercedes-Benz have not always made it easy for their fans. Look back into

the 1950s: The 300 SLR appeared then. These three letters sufficed to transmit both its task and message: They stand for sport, lightness, racing.

In fact, the 300 SLR is a car that intoxicates. The racing sports car won the Mille miglia, the Targa Florio, the Tourist Trophy, and the Eifelrennen—basically everything that had a rank and a name. In the end it gave its builders the victory in the World Sports Car Championship.

And then Rudolf Uhlenhaut, passenger-car test chief and technical leader of the racing department, delivered. He combined the successful racing sports car with an everyday body reminiscent of the 300 SL. He even got road permission for it. It is an unbelievable automobile—with just one fundamental weakness: Mercedes-Benz built only two examples of the 300 SLR. They were not for sale. For series production of an extreme sports car, as Mercedes-Benz saw it, the time was not yet right.

Over the decades, little changed in this attitude, as much as fans regretted it. Surely there was always something desirable—the most popular were the C 111 models (as of 1969) or the C 112 (1991). But they did not make it to the dealers' showrooms. Affluent fans sent blank checks to Stuttgart-Untertuerkheim, but in vain. Even money cannot persuade anybody there.

The front of the SLR McLaren reminds one of the design of the Formula I Silver Arrows.

The first light on the horizon, the CLK-GTR, appeared in 1997. Mercedes-Benz promised that there would be a small series of 25 cars. Good news—even if that cannot meet the demand by a long shot. After years of abstinence, Mercedes-Benz was coming back to the top class of international motorsport for all to see: At the end of 1998 Mika Hakkinen would become Formula I World Champion for McLaren-Mercedes.

The atmosphere in the firm's headquarters again seemed to be more open to those extroverted subjects to which a supercar belongs. Early rumors turn up, saying that it is only a matter of time before Mercedes-Benz closes this long-ignored gap, in which both sales and image matter.

In the middle of this vacuum, the overture to the SLR-McLaren chapter rings out. At the Detroit Motor Show in January 1999 it became obvious how Mercedes-Benz regarded the future of supercars. The place was chosen deliberately, for the Daimler-Chrysler firm had been founded just a year before. In Detroit there is a suitable frame for the first appearance of the "Vision SLR," as Mercedes calls its idea of a supercar for the coming twenty-first century. The very name builds a bridge: In this "show car," as Daimler Chrysler calls it, styling elements from Mika Hakkinen's victorious car mix with the classic form of the 1955 300 SLR.

The concept excites many fans. Even the young ones, who never actually saw or heard the original 300 SLR in action. They immediately get the message of the "Vision SLR." The strong lines and deliberately pointed proportions with the extremely long hood (23 centimeters [9 inches] longer than on the SL), small passenger space (13 centimeters [5 inches] shorter), and strikingly angular rear create a Silver Arrow for tomorrow with the understanding of yesterday. The form also conveys the clear message that makes the progressive technology of the car known.

Fortunately, neither basic practicability nor conservative restraint dictates limits to the vehicle. Quite the opposite: The show car expresses the pure joy of the automobile, combined with everything that was applicable to future technology in 1999. The "Vision SLR" may strike a blow for freedom from the chains of the mass market, an attempt to break loose and move upward and thus initiate a sort of catharsis for the brand: Mercedes-Benz is inventing a supercar for its fans anew.

The "Vision SLR" began as a study in 1999.

Loaded with technology and design: The SLR McLaren is also big on image.

One cannot do the job in a small way, as those responsible for the project at Mercedes-Benz know. For now the new, unfamiliarly wide roof of Daimler Chrysler extends over them. They want to play at the top of the big league, and speak with no false modesty of the "technological leadership in auto building."

So the supercar design appears very self-conscious, "pregnant, but the Vision SLR does not flex muscles aggressively," Mercedes-Benz writes in the press kit for its debut—it offers a "contrasting play of sharply drawn lines and soft shapes." The front end stands out with its Hakkinen nose. Instead of wearing one of the familiar Mercedes radiator masks, the SLR's front end is shaped like an arrow. The element of double wings is added, clearly developing their own formal concept that is repeated in the most varied places in the body and interior—for example, between the headlights and front apex, most noticeably on the sides, the air intakes of the engine hood, or the steps of the outer shape.

So everything is very different, and yet the "Vision SLR" is still a Mercedes-Benz. For the four-eye headlight design that was introduced in the E-Class in 1995 makes the family membership clear at first glance, even though it appears here in a new, unfamiliar form. In the "Vision SLR" each pair of eyes blend into a unit without giving up their basic oval form.

Along with these clear signs of modern styling, the design also reaches back to some ideas of times gone by. The strikingly long engine hood is also part of this, as is the accentuated sweep that lies above the fenders. And to a particular extent, it is the doors that unmistakably link the "Vision SLR" with its ancestors. The wing doors, swinging far into the sky have been a *non plus ultra* of automotive styling since they first appeared in 1952, spectacular and unmistakable.

In the "Vision SLR" the doors are attached to the front roof pillars and swing upward a voluptuous 75 degrees.

In the rear area the "Vision SLR" departed clearly from its model. Here it became modern for pragmatic reasons. The rear was high, but the sideline swung out dynamically. Mercedes-Benz spoke of the "formal uncoupling of the rear fender from the trunk lid." For only a high rear brings a tangible mass to depart—and thus more stability.

The chassis, once welded into a tubular frame, is made of carbon fiber and aluminum in the "Vision SLR." It offers the passengers optimal protection, and yet it is light—carbon fiber saves up to 50% the weight of steel. Depending on the function of a component, the designers chose either aluminum or carbon fiber. For example, in the front part of the body are crumple zones that are programmed to be crushed. Aluminum can handle this task best.

The cockpit, on the other hand, is carefully built of carbon fiber material. It promises extreme firmness—a quality that maintains a safe survival space in a collision. Thus the focus of the "Vision SLR" is not only on sportiness, but also on sturdy construction. As for safety, it allows no tolerance, as the protection from accidents involving "lateral pole whiplash" shows. It ranks among the most extreme pressures that a body can be exposed to. Thanks to a highly rigid door-sill design, in which an energy-absorbing foam material is enclosed for completion, the passengers themselves are then optimally protected if they crash sideways into a pole or tree in an accident.

The very modern carbon fiber materials stand out for their excellent energy absorption values, which are four to five times better than those of metallic materials. Since this technology, with its excellent crash stability, was introduced in Formula I racing, the risk of injury has decreased markedly.

The designers of the "Vision SLR" have worked on the subject of lighting as well. For up to five degrees, the projection headlights automatically follow the steering. Thus the light is where the driver needs it.

Along with the low- and high-beam lights, both of xenon quality, the fog lights and the directionals, the "Vision SLR" offers two spotlights with a long range. There is also a light for city driving. The taillights are located as an LED design—in 1999 a highly modern, futuristic subject—on two free-standing wing profiles, one above the other.

When the model was displayed in Detroit, the press realized that the "Vision SLR" wanted to be more than just an exciting car to look at. It is a matter of driving. A quick look at the configuration of the engine shows that. For under the long front hood is the highly developed V-8 engine from the Mercedes S-Class, which the engineers brought

There must be some display. The doors provide the showiness.

The picture deceives: The SLR McLaren is not for romantics.

Such futuristic technology shows the value that the "Vision SLR" has for Daimler Chrysler. It was developed as a thorough concept, as shown by the care which Mercedes-Benz devoted to the interior. The supercar of the future looks pure: no cloth, no wool. Only the top panel and the roof pillars are still covered with webbing. A central element is formed by the wide central console into which the striking nose of the "Vision SLR" continues. A back that structures the engine hood unites the two elements.

It is no surprise that behind the steering wheel, which is formed as an oval, there is no usual instrument panel in the cockpit. Instead, silver wing profiles take the central SLR motif higher up. The two round aluminum-framed instruments remind one of classic, high-value chronometers. Yet it is no surprise that the technology is completely modern. Thus displays are set in the center where the driver has an unspoiled view because the needles are located on transparent plastic discs.

The extreme bucket seats are made of carbon fiber. Their conception comes directly from racing. For the first time with such a design, a special multi-layered fiber structure allows for individual settings for the seat inclination, even though the seat is one piece. The length and height, though, are electrically adjustable, as usual, but there are additional spring damper units under the seats that eliminate swinging and jolting.

What many had long predicted, many hoped for, and some few were supposed to be made happy by was announced by Daimler Chrysler officially on July 9, 1999: The SLR is coming! The news almost sounded solemn: "With the decision on the production start of the Mercedes-Benz SLR, the Stuttgart automobile marquee returns to the top class of the supercar." The marketing detectives had actually found a small but sufficient niche in the market. "The segment of high-value sports cars," according to a press release, would "almost double yearly worldwide to about 2,500 automobiles." And Daimler Chrysler thus set its goal—it would like 20% of the market. Besides the main markets of Europe, the United States, and Japan, the Near and Middle East were envisioned.

to a new level of evolution for use in the "Vision SLR." With 5.5-liter displacement, and a compact supercharger located between the cylinder banks, the three-valve engine with phase-delayed double ignition supplies a lavish 557 hp. At 4,000 rpm it already produces the maximum torque of 720 Nm. It already has a lot of power farther down: At 2,000 rpm the data sheets already promise 580 Nm. A five-speed automatic transmission sends the power along.

The brake system of the "Vision SLR" is best equipped for the performance of the supercharged V-8 engine, even under hard use and extreme pressure. The discs consist of fiber-reinforced ceramic, a material that is not only two-thirds lighter than gray, cast iron but also very heat-resistant. Stable at 1,000 degrees, it copes with temperatures that may be twice as high as ordinary brake-disc material. This provides tremendous safety reserves for sharp braking from high speed.

Civil—and wild. But the SLR McLaren defends itself against categorization.

Juergen Hubbert, than in charge of the Mercedes-Benz passenger cars, was sure of himself: "The Mercedes-Benz SLR," he said, will "become a pattern for the sports car of the twenty-first century." The declared goal was to adopt technology and images from Formula I racing in a small series.

In production there would be "close cooperation" with McLaren Cars, Ltd. In 1995 there had been an association between Mercedes-Benz and McLaren. The British firm wanted to invest 200 million Euros along with the German-American company to build a new factory in Woking, in southern England, for SLR production at the McLaren Technology Centre. Daimler Chrysler took a 40% part in the complex, half of which would be used to produce the SLR McLaren, while the other half would be used for Formula I activities.

Here 140 highly qualified workers were to build 500 vehicles per year. In 2003, as it was planned, the supercar would come onto the market. Ron Dennis, the chief at McLaren, spoke enthusiastically of excitement, perfection, fascination. Mercedes-Benz, too, did not pile it on too high, and announced the SLR as "a Mercedes synthesis of legend and innovation, impressive in every aspect." And they cheerfully went on with the theme in the marketing strategies: In the autumn of 1999, a good half-year after the first public appearance of the SLR, and still long before production would begin, Daimler-Chrysler showed a second version of the "Vision SLR." At the Frankfurt IAA the supercar was shown as a roadster.

The complexity of the program was shown when some four years went by before the first customer could finally receive his hotly desired SLR. There is much more experience involved in beginning series production of cars that are produced conventionally in great numbers than in starting a small series that must live up to all Mercedes-Benz standards. It begins with the fact that from the "Vision SLR" an automobile was developed that also corresponded with envisioned driving qualities. The designers lengthened the wheelbase a mighty 20 centimeters (~8 inches), so that the V-8 supercharger could move back behind the front axle.

This SLR McLaren is typically Mercedes-Benz, and yet completely different.

Production experts also tried to automate the CFK structures considerably more than was formerly possible. Instead of wasting time with laminating by hand, they adapted special processes from aircraft technology like highly firm adhesion and special riveting technology. But classic procedure used for textiles also opens new possibilities—the high-tech material was now sewn, knitted, woven, and plaited. It was the very first time that carbon fibers were used in automobile production to a large extent—plus as a load-bearing structure. As suggested by the "Vision SLR," even crash elements consisted of carbon fibers. In a head-on collision, for example, two conical structures absorb the entire crash energy. Despite their length of 62 centimeters (~25 inches), they weighed only 3.4 kg (7.5 lbs).

On September 8, 2003, the SLR McLaren could finally celebrate its world premiere—not in Stuttgart or Detroit, not in England where it was built, and not on a closed race course. The supercar made its first appearance in Brescia, a north Italian city that generally is not a center of world's attention. But there, 48 years before, Stirling Moss had started on his legendary Mille Miglia. In a 300 SLR he covered the roughly 1,600-kilometer (~995 miles) road race to Rome and back in only ten hours and barely eight minutes. With an average speed of 157.6 kph (~98 mph), it was an all-time record. Juan Manuel Fangio finished second, likewise in a Mercedes-Benz 300 SLR.

From that Piazza Vittorio in the heart of Brescia, where Moss and Fangio started in their 300 SLRs in 1955, the first production SLR started on its first run, which took it not to Rome, but directly to the IAA in Frankfurt. Stirling Moss traveled to Brescia once again, and Formula 1 star Kimi Raikkonen sat at the wheel of the SLR McLaren. He drove the new car over the Stilfser Joch with its 87 hairpin turns, and late at night they reached AMG in Affalterbach. The next morning the public in Frankfurt saw the first edition of the production SLR.

"Unmistakably a Mercedes, but with proportions as if in a distortion mirror. On this engine hood a helicopter could land," wrote *auto motor und sport* about the unusually shaped SLR McLaren in issue 10 (2004). And "a cocktail that takes your breath away—strong in aroma, angled in aftertaste." An expensive

drink, for the originally stated price of €375,000 (~$470,000) had meanwhile risen to €435,000 (~$540,500). Whoever ordered everything, including the big wheels, got a bill for €455,300 (~$570,000). Included in the price was picking up the car in the SLR Experience Center in Woking, naturally with orientation and seat fitting. How expensive that was is shown by comparing it with the SL 65 AMG, which at €201,840 (~$251,000) cost less than half, without being much weaker with its 612 hp.

But the production SLR was not just more expensive than had been announced, but also stronger. Instead of 577 hp, it now produced 626 hp at 6,500 rpm. Mercedes-AMG had optimized the new performance of the V-8 from the SL 55 AMG and given it a compact, modern screw supercharger between the two banks of cylinders. Depending on the engine speed and pressure on the engine, an electromagnetic clutch shifted it in fractions of a second. Rebuilding to dry-sump lubrication had been demanding, while omitting the oil pan let the engine

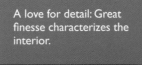

A love for detail: Great finesse characterizes the interior.

sit lower in the chassis. The SLR car had become a strong character. Despite plenty of high-tech bells and whistles, one need not see it is a high-strung, highly sensitive mechanical work. It presents itself quite differently. "A bolt of power, a primal beast, a grandiose piece of technology that, with all its good disposition has shown a primordial character," as *auto sport* characterized it.

Since 1999 the majority owner of AMG has been Daimler Chrysler, and in Affalterbach, Swabia, the SLR engines are built by hand—"One man, one motor" is the concept. A single mechanic takes on the complete assembly of an engine from the first to the last screw. It is a delicate job: Forged blocks with forged, lightly made pistons are used. Every part is measured, weighed, and located exactly. But the SLR McLaren only becomes a car in Woking.

Thus high tech is used as never before in production auto building. The link between the past and future is made by the air brake. On heavy braking, the rear spoiler automatically rises to an angle of 65 degrees. A load of up to 167 kilograms (368 lbs) is added to the rear axle, and the higher air resistance provides active brake support. Something similar, though in a technically simpler way, was offered in 1955 by one variant of the original SLR.

The SLR McLaren can be started with a small button. It is located on the shift lever, under a small flap—as if there were a danger of pushing it by accident. "Like the machine-gun trigger in a jet fighter," said *sport auto* (#6, 2004). The experts were also surprised at how rough, almost brutal the naturally quite civilized 90-degree V-8 seems. And when the supercharger cuts in, the SLR McLaren shrieks and yowls and drives "fear into the limbs" of the unfamiliar, which really pleased the folks at *sport auto:* "With its dark-colored, sharply contoured engine sound, the SLR V-8 could win almost any noise contest." All the more so because it growls out of striking side exhaust pipes. Who else can offer such a thing? And no, that is not half-grown. Mercedes names other reasons: Naturally, an aura of reminiscence, because it was formerly like that with the 300 SLR. But above all because a typical exhaust system would have cut through the smooth bottom of the car and limited the effect of the diffuser.

But Horst von Saurma, the *sport auto* journalist, also defuses the magic of the Mercedes-Benz mythos that envelops the SLR McLaren: "Technologically it has neither anything in common with its oft-cited predecessor from the fifties," he wrote, "nor does it present a parallel technology with the Formula I Silver Arrows." Perhaps, *sport auto* suggests, Mercedes-Benz simply could have set the marketing level a little lower: Then the "expectations would be reduced to what the SLR is actually capable of accomplishing in its very individual character."

In the "Supertest" Horst von Saurma approaches the SLR McLaren very critically. "A pure racing sports car that sharpens its profile only from success on the race track basically looks different." For a front engine is unusual for a supercar, even if it—and there is praise for it—was pushed far back from the front axle toward the middle of the car. This change results in the relatively long wheelbase of 2,700 millimeters (106 inches). No wonder that the SLR McLaren glows in an excellent straight-ahead run. That the curve speeds are also high is owed to its large track width—and the light, highly modern design of its axles made mainly of carefully cast aluminum parts and, as for the transverse links, of forged aluminum. In front a quadruple-link axle is used; in back, multi-links guide the wheels.

How difficult the fine line is in tuning the chassis of a supercar is shown in the contradicting reactions. On the one hand, good suspension comfort is wanted, even though it does not apply in every sense to luxury *Gran Turismo* chassis. Whoever wants to be really fast finds too many compromises in the SLR McLaren—even if it is only the weight, which includes luxuriously equipping the car with separately controlled automatic air conditioning and a Bose sound system. Even an automatic baby-seat system is featured in the standard SLR equipment. It turns off the air bag, while the belt tightener and sidebag remain active. But does a person who likes to drive fast actually have small children on board?

On the subject of speed-dependent steering, too, the supercar takes some getting used to. The geared-rod steering is laid out relatively pointed. It is more than precise, meaning nervous and very direct.

On the race course in particular, it is difficult to find the right line, because—with ESP turned off, of course—one has to keep the rear axle permanently under control, as it tends to step off to the left or right from the overabundance of power. The autobahn makes it feel more at home than the mountain pass does.

But whoever is looking for a nervous stomach will find it: "It is a fascination to see how problem-free the brachial power is put on the road," *sport auto* praises.

Auto motor und sport reports on the "staccato of the anti-skid regulation": The SLR McLaren grabs at curves as if "it needed to tear up the asphalt."

The five-speed automatic transmission, rather a surprise in a sports car, works inconspicuously but very convincingly. It can be programmed by a switch to "sport," "supersport," or "race." Thus the SLR McLaren is always able to lap the north section of the Nuerburgring in 7.52 minutes. That is a respectable time, all the more so because one never sets his/her demands on his/her driving skill too high. "To unchain its primal powers, it is enough to press the gas pedal into the floor covering. The technology takes care of everything else," Wolfgang Koenig notes in *auto motor und sport; sport auto* takes up the same theme: "The SLR reveals itself—very cleverly in marketing technique—to a very select public that has already rejected tough advertising but does not want to do without the related thrill." Or in other words, even the untalented can play with 626 hp here without immediately injuring themselves or others.

But there is something more to it: As of July 2006, the special SLR McLaren 722 model became available. The "722" refers to the legendary original SLR in which Stirling Moss won the 1955 Mille Miglia. Every car then bore the starting number that indicated its starting time—and the Moss-Jenkinson team started the race at 7:22 A.M. With 25 more horsepower and 44 kilograms (97 lbs) less weight, the Super-SLR is just a bit faster, and has Brembo-carbon brakes and optimized running gear laid out considerably more sportingly.

In the autumn of 2007 there was another increase: The SLR McLaren GT, limited to 21 cars, served as a racing version for use in the SLR Club Trophy races. As specialists, the RML Group took over the production of this version, which weighed in at only 1,390 kg (3,064 lbs). The advantage in numbers: With 680 hp, now 3.0 seconds suffice for the sprint from zero to 100 kph (0 to 62 mph).

Anyone for whom all of this was fast enough, but somehow too limited, could turn to the roadster as of 2007. Eight years (!) after the car's first presentation, it was ready to sell—for €493,850 (~$678,400). The designers had to change some

The new car has no retro design. But a touch of the classics is in it.

500 parts for the open version. For example, the rimless doors and the attachment points of the seat belts were new. Only the body structure itself, usually a main theme in coupes that were opened later, scarcely needed any extensions; it was already extremely stiff as it was.

The SLR project ended at the end of 2009. Insiders suspect that it was not paying its way. Of the announced 3,500 cars to which Mercedes-Benz had limited this model, probably no more than about 1,700 were built—still an excellent number in the supercar class. Without a doubt, the SLR McLaren has fulfilled its task: It has shown how Mercedes-Benz defined the concept of the supercar at the beginning of the twenty-first century—and pushed many limits. At the same time, it rolled out the red carpet for the successful SLS AMG project, which was to begin in 2009.

A car like the SLR McLaren is not the type that would let its life end with a whimper. No, it was still beating the drum: SLR McLaren Stirling Moss was the name of the final series, limited to 75 cars, that was built as a link with the last regular roadster. The price of this fifth SLR version was a mighty €892,500 (~$1.2 million). For this high price, the buyer went without a roof and a windshield—and received one of the most extreme automobiles on the market, with 650 hp, 350 kph (217 mph) top speed, and two minimal wind deflectors instead of a windshield. "So open and at the same time so fast is no other production car," said Mercedes-Benz.

The split of the SLR was mighty. For many manufacturers can build a beast of a car. Many can also build a luxurious car. But this high-tech mixture, loaded with historic motorsport success, could come only from Mercedes-Benz.

"One understands everything, one finds everything, everything completely normal," tester Wolfgang Koenig wrote, and brought the character to the fore: "Outside a monster, inside a Mercedes, that is calming."

Technical Data

Make	Mercedes-Benz
Model	SLR McLaren
Years Built	2004-2009
Number Built	~2,000
Engine Type	V-8, 5,439 cc (332 cu in), 460 kW (626 hp) at 6,500 rpm
Gearbox	5-speed automatic
Top Speed	334 kph (~208 mph)
Dimensions	wheelbase 2,700 mm (106 inches)
Weight	1,768 kg (3,897 lbs)

A DTM Racing Car for the Street

At first glance it looks very proper, perhaps slightly tuned. But the reality looks different. The road-usable DTM derivative provides unlimited driving fun. The quantity made, of course, is strictly limited.

I t does not betray everything when one looks at its tail. On the left, "CLK" is lettered, on the right, "AMG." But what enlivens the whole thing, the idea behind it, is not documented on the sheet metal: the three letters DTM, short for Deutsche Tourenwagen Masters, which this car bears in the middle of its name.

CLK DTM AMG. Never has a Mercedes-Benz had a stranger name, and its appearance is also very unusual. In street traffic it seems familiar at the first moment, until one realizes what one is seeing. It is as if an eloquent business-lady appeared at a meeting, dressed in nice clothes above and skin-tight athletic clothes and spike heels below. This CLK is charming, beyond a doubt, with major contrasts. "Whoever doesn't want to be noticed, drives at night," said Goetz Leyrer in 2004 in *auto motor und sport*.

The cryptic name is thoroughly correct, for the CLK DTM AMG means nothing else but a mixture of the sporting and elegant CKM touring coupe and a racing car to DTM specifications, cheerfully prepared by the firm's motorsport specialists, AMG. The contract contained it; it was supposed to turn the extreme CLK into nothing less than a road-usable version of the most successful participant in the German Touring Car Masters, a notorious production-car victor and superior

Mastery winner of the 2003 season. In this second season, the racing CLK, driven by Bernd Schneider and Christijan Albers, among others, finished first in all ten races.

A CLK, tuned: In appearance the CLK DTM AMG sticks together.

With so much success and its effect on the public, it seems like an alluring idea to build this proven racing car in civilized form as a small series for collectors. The basis was the large-series CLK, but the result had not much to do with it except the desired visual recognition. The otherwise excellent CLK body appeared wide here, very wide, completely following the style of the DTM racing touring car. Its fenders stick their elbows into its hips mightily, and it cowers lowly on the road. In front, gigantic openings suck in great quantities of cooling air; in back a high-tech spoiler reigns, unbeautified and bold, over the trunk lid. The steering is convincingly efficient; at 200 kph (124 mph) more than 36 added kilograms (~80 lbs) press on the rear axle and contribute to driving stability. Further down, the rear skirt reveals typical diffuser structures.

This somewhat riotous appearance does not please everyone. "There is a lot of show in the "CLK DTM AMG," Goetz Leyrer notes in *auto motor und sport* on the appearance of this extreme coupe.

As an example of this, Leyrer cites the ventilation louvers in the fender widenings, which have no actual function. The steering wheel, flattened above and below, could only get by as a styling trick in view of the lavish spaciousness of the cockpit.

Whoever has a sporting task to fulfill usually considers his weight. So does the CLK DTM AMG. What is not necessary—away with it! For instance, the rear seat. Why have seats ready in the back for passengers who are not going to sit there anyway? Besides, many body and interior components are made of the especially light, yet all the more stable, carbon-fiber bonding material CFK.

That despite these measures, the CLK DTM AMG does not manage to distance itself clearly from the weight discipline of a production CLK is due, for one thing, to various racing specifications. For example, the high consumption of more than 17 liters per 100 kilometers (~14 mpg), which impelled the responsible parties to install an additional 30-liter (8 gallons) tank over the rear axle to add to the 62-liter (16 gallons) standard

So civilized, so fast: Mercedes-Benz CLK DTM AMG.

tank. This solution is helpful, though so pragmatic and commonplace that it is remarkable in a supercar. Then, too, the engine, now fitted with a supercharger, increases the car's empty weight; so do the big wheels with brakes to match, and the fact that customers, even in a supercar with DTM genes, no longer get along without comfortable extras like automatic air conditioning.

The AMG racing experts could not work magic on the absolute weight. Yet they divided the weight evenly on the two axles: 54% in front, 46% in back. Since the screw supercharger with its necessary cooling technology added some weight to the engine compartment, the battery and the windshield washer had to be moved to the back.

The CLK DTM racing touring car of the 2003 season.

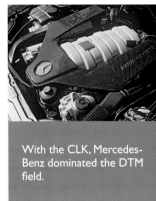

With the CLK, Mercedes-Benz dominated the DTM field.

In front, under the CLK hood, power lurks. Who can claim to have, as a result of its tuning measures, an engine like the 5.5-liter, AMG V-8, such as powers, for example, the SL 55 AMG? The CLK DTM AMG can: Thanks to the supercharger pressure, with its special low-temperature air cooler, its peak performance climbs to 582 hp. It is no less impressive than its torque, with its peak at more than 690 N/m (509 lb-ft) spreads out on a plateau: At just 2,000 rpm it shakes 690 N/m out of its sleeves; at 2,500 rpm it has reached 750 N/m (553 lb-ft), and at the end of the range, at 7,000 rpm, the V-8 still supplies almost 600 N/m (442 lb-ft).

Thus it is no wonder that this coupe not only looks fast, but also runs fast. At all levels, the CLK DTM AMG moves along mightily. "Every step on the gas pedal," Goetz Leyrer praises, the CLK answers "with an infernal push." And his colleague, sport-auto tester Marcus Schurig, writes that this engine is a "puller before the Lord."

With it, the driver is best armed for all demands of everyday and other situations; in 3.9 seconds the CLK DTM AMG sprints from zero to 100 kph (0 to 62 mph), and reaches 200 kph (124 mph) in 10.9 seconds. And it keeps going until it reaches its peak at 320 kph (~200 mph). No, the air does not come out of it yet. It is the electronics that bar its way—presumably so that the wild CLK does not take the prize away from its partner, the SLR, *en passant*. "The acceleration takes place according to a digital pattern," Goetz Leyrer describes the

characteristics of the CLK DTM AMG: "Give it gas and the desired speed is reached." Even at its top speed the car runs "just as stable as an oil tanker." A lap on the north Nuerburgring, the measure of all sports cars to be taken seriously, takes the CLK DTM AMG 7.54 minutes. That is respectable, for the least expensive Mercedes SLR McLaren, which cost €200,000 (~$250,000 in 2004) did it only two seconds faster. For Marcus Schurig, the *sport auto* man, the verdict is sure: "The CLK DTM AMG is the real supercar from Mercedes, let the marketing strategists say what they please."

The engineers at Mercedes-AMG can write on their banners that it has done well. After all, they have 35 years of racing and developing high-performance engines behind them, and so they planned the necessary measures with a sure hand: They strengthened the crankcase again, made forged pistons of highly specialized material, reworked the

The master and his car: Bernd Schneder in the 2003 CLK DTM.

exhaust camshaft so that the valve opening times became longer and improved filling the combustion chambers. The better ducting of the intake air did its part to improve performance just as the faster-turning screw supercharger did. And to complete the new work environment, the engine electronics are completely devoted.

Now that sounds rather academic. The real goose-bumps, though, come when the eight cylinders begin to breathe. Tester Marcus Schurig reported in *sport auto* on the idling behavior: "The motor rumbled like a cold racing motor with a sharp screeching wave in the eighties." The press kit, obligated to use sober words, informs: "Purest motor-sport flair is incorporated in the sound of the AMG motor." And admits that the sound design was in the picture. "Thanks to its fully newly developed AMG sport exhaust system, the unmistakable sound recalls the successful racing touring cars from the DTM."

And it penetrates, along with a crowd of vibrations, unfiltered into the cabin to the passengers. If the wrong people have strayed into the CLK DTM AMG, then the unsmoothed advent of the V-8 supercharger should inspire them: It "sharpens every mountain, goes like hell and roars like a racing car," Marcus Schurig wrote in a *sport auto* supertest in 2004.

A plate on the supercharger of the engine documents its origin. But there is not just the maker's name, but—true to the AMG philosophy of "one man, one motor"—the signature of its builder. At

the engine factory he has "under great ability of his hands at special workplaces" assembled the engine from individual components.

An automatic gearbox handles the power transmission, even though the "tiny shift lever on the central console," as Goetz Leyrer noted critically in *auto motor und sport,* "suggests the presence of a sequential gearshift." In a supercar, automatic transmission always inspires distanced commentary, even though they bear impressive names like "AMG Speedshift" and can be shifted manually by steering-column paddles: right up, left down. The shifting times are made extremely short. "The engine hangs on the gas as with a mechanical clutch," Goetz Leyrer wrote; "The shifting processes take place quickly and noisily."

After the engine starts, the manual shift mode is always active. But whoever wants to can drive the CLK DTM AMG with automatic transmission as calmly as a taxi. Nothing can go wrong; that is typical of Mercedes-Benz. For the tachometer shows the actual engine speed via 64 light diodes; their color changes from white to red as the top engine speed of 7,000 rpm is approached as a friendly hint from the system about the now-missing gear shift. Intervention does nothing; whoever remains stubborn and lets it come sends the engine to the end of the tachometer as he watches. But Goetz Leyrer sees it as a fault that the automatic transmission, when being downshifted, cannot give gas in between, as sequential shifts master it so perfectly.

AMG also offers a convertible version.

That is inviting: It's a pleasant ride in the open CLK DTM AMG.

The motorsport specialist Mercedes-AMG also worked intensively on the running gear. They succeeded, tester Goetz Leyrer found: "For in handling the CLK is the king. It seems to be grown together with the road." And Marcus Schurig of *sport auto* sees it similarly: "The steering behavior is almost a sensation. The CLK throws itself into every curve with a directness and precision that makes you think you are in a racing car."

Instead of earlier leaf springs, a height-adjustable screw suspension is used, allowing a very exact adjustment of the vehicles height. The rear axle also has completely new spring links and strengthened wheel carriers that provide better traction and longer standing time. AMG has strengthened all the rubber elements, and the attachment of the shock absorbers to the body is done by uniball elements that come from auto racing and allow a very precise driving operation. To reduce the sideways tendency in fast curves, the CLK DTM AMG has a harder rear-axle stabilizer than the production model.

All of this is very successful, Goetz Leyrer found: "How perfect the tuning of the home-developed screw suspension is can also be seen when one takes one's foot off the gas. And suddenly finds: This is not only a racing car, this is also a Mercedes. No tough racer, but a coupe thoroughly suitable for touring." Marcus Schurig, his *sport auto* colleague, agrees: "No dull I-have-the-wildest-

racing-suspension opinion, no retesting of the ability to suffer, no crudeness." There is even some of the "typical Mercedes gentleness" to feel. "If one would not look at one's fellow men so comically, everything would be as usual."

With 582 hp and 800 N/m (590 lb-ft), traction is a central theme. Here a lamellar differential lock on the rear axle helps the CLK DTM AMG; it functions by the same principle as in the DTM racing touring car. It locks 60% pulling and 40% pushing. And since the rear axle has to work a lot in action, it has its own oil cooler.

To be able to control the high performance safely, the AMG Mercedes retains the dependable standard systems like the drive slide regulation (ASR) and the electronic stability program (ESP) on board. To be sure, they are tuned to the new work environment. So the ESP allows "the rear end a happy life of its own before the stabilizing braking occurs," says *auto motor und sport* tester Goetz Leyrer. The ESP regulation "occurs late here, is sensitive and extremely active," says his colleague Marcus Schurig.

And whoever trusts himself can also turn off the ESP. Then the CLK DTM AMG offers a "purposeful amount of oversteer," as the press kit carefully formulates. For "inspiring agility and highest driving dynamics" means, above all, that wild drifts are the order of the day. Goetz Leyrer has tried it out: "On normal roads, even when they are dry and easy to grip, the avoidance of the suspension electronics is like that of a juggler with a live hand grenade."

The optional Dunlop "Super sport Race" tires contribute their own share to the performance of the CLK DTM AMG. Thanks to their special rubber mix and asymmetrical profile, the tires really bite into the asphalt—up to 1.35 g of lateral acceleration are in them. That is far more than is to be justified outside a race course. And the Dunlop Super Sport Race tires like moisture so little that a label in the cockpit warns of the results.

The 19- and 20-inch aluminum wheels provide enough space for a lavishly dimensioned braking system in bonding technology. It saves about 20% of the weight and heightens the thermal strength, because the gray metal discs are bonded axially and radially with aluminum bowls. Though the brake system is set up for optimal firmness, perfect behavior under pressure and equal dosage, the brake assistance from the production cars is retained. Mercedes-AMG has suited it to the new conditions.

That also applies to the driver's cockpit. It is strikingly functional, all black with various coverings made of CFK, the carbon-fiber bonding material. The leather-covered sport bucket seats also consist of this light material, and the CLK DTM AMG has two, four-point belts that give the passengers perfect lateral support and protection. The driver steers with an oval, thick wild-leather wheel. Any asceticism? Only on the highest level. That is also true because Bi-zenon headlights, the Keyless-Go keyless operation system, and a radio with a navigation system are on board, and the Mercedes-AMG specialists are always open to further wishes. "No, there is no scrimping here," Marcus Schurig comments in *sport auto*: "That was infernally expensive."

What does such an automobile lack but a few drops of vermouth? Not much. Perhaps only the fact that the CLK DTM AMG was limited to 100 specimens. And collectors had secured them even before the first one was built in the autumn of 2004, despite a price of €236,060 ($291,612).

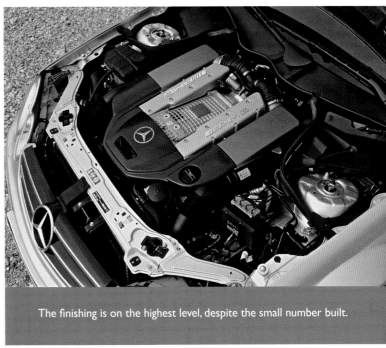

The finishing is on the highest level, despite the small number built.

Technical Data

Make	Mercedes-Benz
Model	CLK DTM AMG
Years Built	2004
Number Built	100
Engine Type	V-8, 5,439 cc (332 cu in), 428 kW (582 hp) at 6,100 rpm
Gearbox	5-speed automatic
Top Speed	320 kph (~200 mph)
Dimensions	wheelbase 2,722 mm (107 inches)
Weight	1,680 kg (3,703 lbs)

Here Comes the Next Act

Mercedes-Benz keeps it coming: The SLS AMG is a pure representative of the supercar class. It inspires testers, convinces fans, and lures buyers. If the SLS AMG did not exist, one would have to invent it. And just exactly as it is.

As if it had always been there: The SLS AMG is convincing.

Yes, it is an absolute eye-catcher. A rock star everywhere. Whoever rolls up to a gas station in one in 2010 must have the nerve to hold a medium press conference. And yes, it is a hell of a joy on the road, this SLS AMG.

A modest two sets of three initials form the code for this new view of supercars that Mercedes-Benz offers. New because this look has moved away from the many extremes that have typified Mercedes-Benz supercars in the last decades. There were faster, more shimmering, rarer, louder, more expensive cars with the star than an SLS AMG. The

only thing that this new Gullwing actually maintains as an extreme is being extremely good. It sounds like a middle ground, an average. And that is simply not the case. Behind the exciting façade of the SLS AMG is a strong character, formed with care, that appears as casual and self-evident as if it had been there for many years. In many ways it is the most convincing Mercedes-Benz sports car that has been around in years, say many testers.

But one thing at a time. A model such as the SLS AMG now embodies was very late. Mercedes-Benz has a glowingly structured array of models with pregnant statistics that are absolutely unmistakable. The S-Class; the E-Class; A-, B-, and C- Classes; plus SL, SLK, R-Class, M-Class, G and GL—the only thing missing is the astonishing, the supercar. They can build high-performance sports cars, as their history since 1900 has proved over and over. A very particular milestone in this unique tradition was the 300 SL of 1954. The legendary gullwing car was a grand master of sporting appearance, a calm opponent of the fastest cars on postwar roads, and yet had that magical *Gran Turismo* atmosphere that made it fit in so perfectly with people in polo shirts, Rodenstock sun glasses, and Dunlop tennis rackets—with wooden frames, naturally. It could do everything, and made a brilliant figure of it. It was not too loud, not too quiet, not too hard, and not too soft—was fast, expensive and exotic, but not too notorious. And yet there was no trace of mediocrity. Even today, far more than half a century after its premiere, one can blame only one thing on it: As a collector's item, it is simply too popular to still be a surprise.

The SLS AMG takes on the typical grille motif again.

Since the era of the 300 SL, gullwing doors have been part of the Mercedes-Benz repertoire.

Its footsteps were ignored for decades. Many regretted this, for example, Bruno Sacco, chief stylist at Mercedes-Benz since 1999. The C 111 could have become a successor, maybe the C 112, too. The SLR, on the other hand, could not, nor the CLK DTM AMG or CLK-GTR—their philosophies were of a different kind.

But now here is the SLS AMG. It has been on our roads since 2010. It is the first model that AMG, once tuner and motorsport specialists and now a branch of the firm, has designed completely on their own. There were many tense questions at first, suspicions, and even confusion. The SLS AMG slipped across the literature and the Internet long before it made its debut. People waited excitedly for it. Accusations of handcrafting errors, as was soon clear, could soon be directed at Mercedes-Benz and AMG.

"Even the dead rise up for it."

Long front end, short tail: The SLS AMG has fascinating proportions.

Mature and wild at the same time: the SLS AMG.

Progress is often found in details: The 571 hp, V-8 engine weighs only 205 kg (~452 lbs).

They made none. Quite the opposite; everything was successful. Their product deludes: "Contact difficulties? Depressions? For €180,000 ($238,552) more? Gullwings up and hop into the cockpit of the Mercedes SLS AMG. Even the dead rise up for it," writes Joern Thomas in *auto motor und sport*.

The SLS AMG has learned a little from the SLR McLaren. The silhouette makes itself remarkable. The front end stretches endlessly long, and from some perspectives it seems to be stretched almost too long. But this length fulfills a function here: For as in the SLR McLaren, the designers have moved the engine far back, to behind the front axle. This position is called front mid-engine. And they have lowered it deep, which works thanks to a height-saving dry-sump lubrication; this was also done in the SLR McLaren. This engine location explains the long wheelbase of 2,680 millimeters (105 inches). In comparison, the Porsche 911 gets by with 2,350 millimeters (~93 inches).

The 6.2-liter, V-8 engine is an old acquaintance in principle. But AMG has reworked the air intake system, valve operation, and camshafts. The designers have unleashed the exhaust system, optimally streamlined the manifolds. Thus the cylinder filling has become clearly better, the engine is more agile and willing to turn than in earlier models. After the cure, the torque rose to 650 N/m (480 lb-ft) at 4,750 rpm, the performance rose 46 hp to 571 hp. That the V-8 engine is long-lived despite its performance is due to the installation of forged pistons, strengthened crankshaft bearings, even the crankcase is clearly reworked. A high-performance oil pump optimizes the oil supply. In this bundle of measures, the eye always spotted a further weight reduction. The potent V-8 weighs only 205 kg (~452 lbs)—that means 360 grams of engine produces one horsepower. An incomparable value.

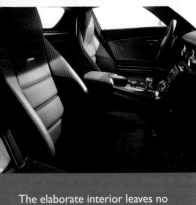

The elaborate interior leaves no doubt about the conception: The SLS AMG is fine for touring.

And it can do a lot, this V-8. The AMG engine reacts to the gas "explosively," *Auto Bild* praises. "When you come off the gas," as Joern Thomas experiences it, the 6.2-liter engine has such a good mood that it "subdues its environment with

AMG developed the SLS, Mercedes-Benz built it.

The SLS AMG does

not have to fear much

competition.

Power source: The V-8 engine comes from the sportsmen at AMG.

growls, snorts, and bangs." And *Auto Bild* writes: "The brutal V-8 motor keeps steam up at any speed, turns aggressively high, the gears shift lightning-fast and neatly without interrupting the propulsion, the thudding hard sound of the big 6.2-liter super sucker gets directly under the skin and into the blood like an adrenaline injection." Georg Kacher, *Auto Bild* tester, even notes that the SLS AMG releases "even when idling, the finery of a badly-built railroad signal box." Or the "hard, mechanical and, at 7,000 rpm, almost painfully impressive spectacle of noise," from which *Auto Bild* reports elsewhere. From *auto motor und sport*, as well, praise comes—from "big block beat," and they thank the developers "that they have lowered this impatient induction engine behind the front axle, and not the V-12 Biturbo powerhouse from the SL 65 AMG. The result would have been a dragster, not a dribbler."

Thus the SLS AMG has little to fear even in the supercar class. In 38.8 seconds it sprints from zero to 100 kph (0 to 62 mph). For short times the lavish engine performance would be sufficient, but not—despite all the treatment—the traction. The electronics end the speed at 317 kph (~195 mph) out of concern for the tires. It is astonishing, too, that such values can be attained by a car that is satisfied to consume an average of 13.2 liters per 100 kilometers (~18 mpg). Even though the

Very different and yet related: Mercedes-Benz 300 SL and SLS AMG.

test consumptions were considerably higher, this value appears very noteworthy in the supercar class. The reasons for it are a series of measures like the friction-optimized LDS layering of the cylinder paths, developed exclusively by AMG. There is also a knowingly regulated oil supply, plus an intelligent generator management that makes sure that at any speed the superfluous engine power is devoted to charging the battery, and not, as otherwise customary, uselessly turned into heat. While accelerating it is just the opposite: There the generator is disconnected, so that in this phase the engine no longer needs to drive it.

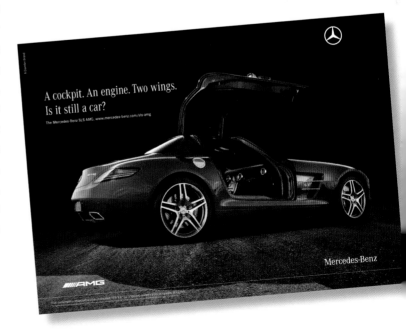

A cockpit. An engine. Two wings.
Is it still a car?

The Mercedes-Benz SLS AMG. www.mercedes-benz.com/sls-amg

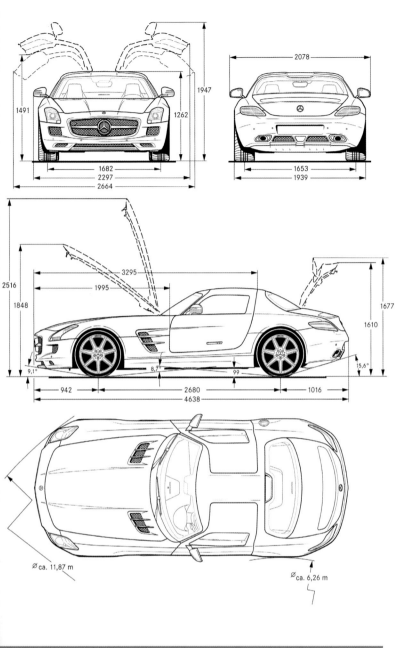

Not visible from outside is the optimal weight division. 47% is in front, 53% in back. This is aided by the fact that the SLS AMG carries its brand-new, seven-speed double-clutch transmission on its rear axle. It comes, incidentally, from the specialist Getrag, which also equips the Ferrari 458 Italia. A tunnel of carbon fiber links the gearbox with the engine. It covers an especially light driveshaft of the same material—a principle that has proved itself in the C-Class DTM touring cars. With four shifting programs, the driver can select the character of the transmission. "Controlled Efficiency" is the name of one, in which the gearbox delivers an extra helping of torque. The "Sport" and especially "Sport Plus" choices, on the other hand, offer high engine speeds. Or the SLS AMG driver can select the seven speeds manually by steering-column paddles. Strong jets of intermediate gas are automatically calculated by the drive software, not only in the "Controlled Efficiency" mode. There it is somewhat more customary.

As the chassis of the SLS AMG, for the first time from Mercedes-Benz, an elaborate aluminum space frame is used. The structure does not admit any unwanted elasticity, the car reacts stiffly, almost twist-free and directly," the press kit explains. The frame consists of 45% aluminum profiles, 31% sheet aluminum, 20% cast aluminum, and only 4% steel. In the A-pillars ultra rigid, heat-shaped special steel is used, which helps to protect the passengers in accidents. The astonishing thing is its slim build: The load-bearing tubular structure weighs only 241 kilograms (531 lbs). With that, along with the engine, it makes an important contribution to the

A classic Gran Turismo—with everything that is now imaginable.

1,620-kilogram (3,571 lbs) entry weight of the SLS AMG. From that a performance weight of only 2.84 kilograms (~6.25 lbs) per horsepower is calculated—compared to other supercars, a very convincing condition.

Now figures alone are not worth much. But Mercedes-AMG has done everything to convert the sober numbers into highly sporting driving qualities. The axles and the power train are attached as deep in the load-bearing structure as possible. That also applies to the bending and momentary stiff transitions of the front and rear of the car to the safe cockpit. The result works out correspondingly: a deep center of gravity and a convincing passage of power through the structure.

The results speak volumes. Thus *Auto Bild* lauds the SLS AMG; it seems "to be sucked firmly onto the asphalt," and determines after test drives on the Contidrom: "Thanks to the extremely low center of gravity and extremely fine balance, the AMG low-flyer even attains higher curve speeds than the Porsche 911 Turbo."

Mercedes-AMG made the suspension, with its aluminum double transverse-link axles, just as important as the steering characteristics. The nervousness that the SLR McLaren still exposed in steering reactions is completely foreign to the SLS AMG.

It remains "on track to the centimeter," says *Auto Bild,* and is to be driven "likewise very roundly with sensible steering-wheel movements." With increasing speed the steering becomes pleasantly stiffer, the contrast to the roadway is excellent. The standard Continental SportContact 5 tires also get much praise.

Large class: The SLS AMG is also suited for relaxed touring.

Not only does the differential lock work safely, so that enough traction is available, the electronic traction control helps out, preventing one of the wheels from turning through brake intervention. Even with the ESP turned off it remains active, which makes the SLS AMG is not only agile but also safe in all situations. "The borderline area is basically defined via the front axle, meaning that it does not proclaim the limit via a rear axle that breaks loose," writes *sport auto*. "Thus the driver can easily judge, via the steering, what he can allow and what he can't."

The ESP is also well thought out. The driver can select the ESP mode with normal corrections or set it on "ESP Sport," which gives him/her somewhat more freedom. If he/she turns the ESP completely off, it is automatically reactivated at the first movement of the brake pedal. The brakes are generously dimensioned and are supported at speeds over 120 kph (~75 mph) by the rear spoiler, which then turns up sharply at once. The

SLS AMG offers a "guillotine brake," says *Auto Bild*. Only at extra cost, to be sure, does one get the implacable but well-regulated ceramic-bonded brakes.

Even critics of the retro wave recognize in the SLS AMG that the designers have combined the chosen genes in a congenial form. Mercedes-Benz understands what the charisma of a 300 SL and a C 111 amount to. They have managed to translate this charisma into a buzzword for the year 2010: "Correct," something the SLS AMG quotes a lot. The grille, with its striking horizontal bar and the chromed SL star in the middle, attracts attention, as do the gullwing doors, which Mercedes-Benz, in a note of serious pragmatism, fashioned so less space is required to open them than usual coupe doors. They can even be opened all the way in a normal garage. Very nice, but how many SLS AMGs will find their home in a normal garage? *Auto Bild* gets to the point: The gullwing doors are simply "pleasure-guiding-responsible." When one gets in over the big, wide door sills, the gullwings help because they reach far into the roof, even though there are cars in the supercar class that let one get in more easily. They are usually opened and closed by muscle power, and they have such

Here something gets cut loose: The SLS AMG in its GT3 version.

as strong, fascinating and alluring effect on the bystanding public, as though a scantily clad Megan Fox has just invited them for a drink.

The fact that the designers did a good job is revealed by the reactions. For the *Auto Bild* Design Award of 2010, some 200,000 readers from 21 European countries voted; the overwhelming winner of the "Most Beautiful Car in Europe" was the SLS AMG. It gathered praise steadily, including the "Red Dot Design Award," the "IF product design award 2010," the "Goldene Lenkrad" *(Auto Bild)* and the "Supersportsman" category in the "Sportiest Cars of 2010" readers' vote *(sport auto)*. The AMG SLS hit the top in form and function, and it does not matter that the name is not a 100% original. The first use of SLS was in 1957 for a racing sports version of the 300 SL roadster, of which only two examples were built and caused a furor in the United States.

Inside the SLS AMG offers what the world expects from a Mercedes-Benz. One sits perfectly, and *sport auto* is enthusiastic about its "handiness, which is revealed by its good visibility, childlike and simple operability, dreamy ergonomics, and last but not least, easy controllability—they mean it can also go slowly. And that with grandeur, acoustically dampened, and properly comfortable despite its sporting suspension." But there is also criticism, as *auto motor und sport* formulates it: "No super-sports-car respect arises," for "the inner appearance does not keep in step with the other one." *Auto Bild* criticizes its "overdrawn instruments," and the aircraft applications are too obvious for some people: too much cockpit, big ducts reminiscent of jet engines, matte metal. The automatic stick shift looks as if one could start an airplane with it.

But the bottom line is that the SLS AMG gets excellent grades in tests, more succinctly than any Mercedes has done for years before it. "Finely dosed," says Joern Thomas in *auto motor und sport* (#16, 2010). The SLS AMG gives off its performance; only the sequential shifting could work a bit more smoothly. The steering is convincing thanks to its precision and spontaneity. Its "finely balanced" chassis is high-class: "Scarcely another supercar is more at home with this satiated, deep-breathing feeling of blending with the road." As to the optional sport chassis, Joern Thomas advises that one should do without it.

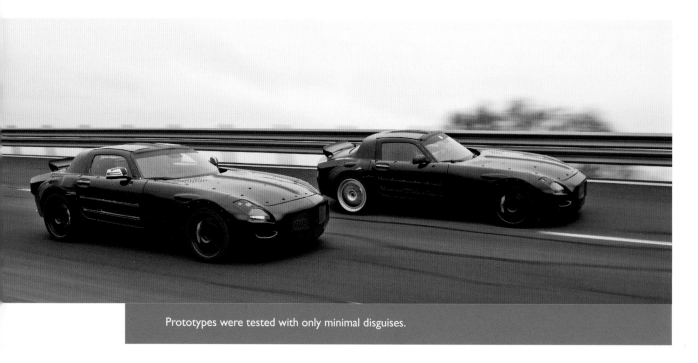

Prototypes were tested with only minimal disguises.

His colleague Horst von Saurma disagrees: Only the version with harder spring characteristics and fitted shock absorbers awakens the racing talent slumbering in the SLS AMG.

Auto Bild is also full of praise. The focal point of the SLS AMG is "tangible somewhere at the manhole cover level." And further: "In scarcely another sports car does the driver feel so close to the road as in the Gullwing." At high speeds, though, the SLS reacts excitedly, "it is quick nevertheless." In issue 27 (2010) it wins the great sports-car comparison: "Just for these doors, we love the Mercedes SLS, with its fat V-8 and knife-sharp handling it also wins first place in the sports-car comparison." The note in issue 23 (2010) is also very clear: "Fifty-six years after the 300 SL, Mercedes proves that it still builds extremely good sports cars," writes Georg Kacher. "The SL is not only an visual highlight, but also a wonderfully balanced driving machine."

In 00:07:40, *sport auto* whipped the SLS AMG around the north course for the "supertest." Whipped? Wrong word: The SLS did it this time fully "as a matter of course." "The system of man and machine forms a constructive symbiosis from the first seat test on, so that good lap times are not the exception but the rule," Horst

von Samura wrote. Only an ABS intervening, somewhat unmotivated, would have prevented an even better result. "The confidence appears at the very first curve," says *sport auto*. And they admit that the SLS AMG has thoroughly amazed the world of sports cars: a "nearly error-free start in a sporting career? That is often accompanied at its start with spite, envy, and mistrust."

Horst von Saurma: "Respect—what the Mercedes sporting branch AMG has put on wheels, is a big show.... The super-sports concept is justified in every way concerning the new SLS AMG.... The concept is not only justified from the viewpoint of the older *Gran Turismo* but also from the standpoint of the practicing sport driver—hats off!" *Auto Bild* puts it scarcely more modestly: "The SLS has everything that it takes to be a sports-car icon. Independent of the gullwing doors, the SLS is exciting."

A lot is going on with the SLS. Over 10,000 of them are to be built, many more than of any other Mercedes-Benz supercar ever before. Direct fuel injection is to come, as is a roadster (necessarily, as with the 300 SL, without gullwing doors)—and even an electric version. "Wings under current," *Auto Bild* called it in June 2010, showing the first SLS AMG E-CELL in fluorescent matte neon yellow, driven by four electric engines located near the wheels—with 533 hp! The gasoline V-8 offers 571 hp, only 38 hp more, but must get along with 230 fewer N/m (170 lb-ft)—the E-Cell offers 880 Nm. And all that without a gearbox. One speed suffices. The AMG technicians did not have to make many changes in the structure, for the SLS developers already had an electric version in mind when they designed the car. The only difference is that mounted on the front axle are flat leaf springs where driveshafts used to be.

Mercedes-Benz put the batteries where the shaft between the engine and gears turns, where the tank and engine would otherwise sit. The trunk remains completely unchanged. AMG has placed 324 lithium-ion cells in three blocks; all told, they hold 48 kilowatt-hours and weigh half a ton. "There complete energy content," Bernhard Schmidt comments in *Auto Bild*, "—please be brave—equals three liters of gasoline." Anyway, its degree of effectiveness is clearly better, around three times so. Yet after 150 average kilometers (93 miles) it is gone. And if one drives for fun, probably around 50 (31 miles). The next charging lasts eight hours until 80% of capacity is reached.

So what? Revolutions sometimes begin that small. This one is stormy already: "No bellowing motor, no pulsating drive train. Out of nothing comes surreal propulsion in over the passengers," Marcus Peters admires in *auto motor und sport:* "One is more shot down than hastened."

The electric SLS moves from zero to 200 kph (0 to 124 mph) in eleven seconds, accompanied only by the whirring of the engines, the driving wind, and tire sound. "In the electric future, sound designers may have much to do with tires and bodies," Schmidt suspects. And Peters writes: "This sound is more than necessary to get used to—one oscillates between fascination and acoustic boredom."

Short driveshafts connect the engines with the wheels. Wheel-hub engines have not been considered because of the high unsprung masses. It rides sensationally, all the more because its center of gravity is even 23 millimeters (~1 inch) lower than in the gasoline version, and because every engine transfers only as much power to its wheel as the tire can use.

With eleven seconds from zero to 200 kph, it is only two-tenths slower than the V-8 version, and that is only at the beginning of its development. It is serious, even the development car is allowed on the road and presents itself as if it would be at the dealer's tomorrow. At the end of 2012, the beginning of 2013, the SLS AMG E-CELL is supposed to go on the market.

And that, 112 years after the original Mercedes was born on Wilhelm Maybach's drawing board, is really a revolution. As it was in 1900. At least.

Technical Data

Make	Mercedes-Benz
Model	SLS AMG
Years Built	2010–
Engine Type	V-8, 6,208 cc (~380 cu in), 420 kW (571 hp) at 6,800 rpm
Gearbox	7-speed double-clutch
Top Speed	317 kph (~195 mph)
Dimensions	wheelbase 2,680 mm (105 inches)
Weight	1,620 kg (3,571 lbs)

Other Schiffer Titles

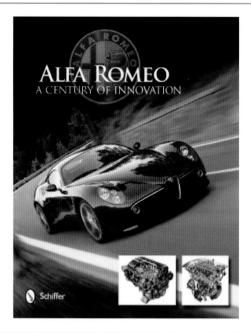

Alfa Romeo: A Century of Innovation. This book documents the fascinating ten-decade history of the Milanese automaker, from the exciting racing and sports cars of the twenties and thirties to the equally advanced and sporty sedans, coupes, and convertibles of the fifties and sixties to the present-day range of technically evolved, innovative vehicles.

Size: 8 1/2 x 11   215 b/w & color photos   136 pp.
ISBN: 978-0-7643-4072-7   hard cover $29.99

The VW Bus: History of a Passion. Jörg Hajt. Author Jörg Hajt portrays VW Transporter buses of all body types, lovingly restored and customized, and offers a comprehensive history of the brand. Nearly 200 archival and modern photos document the wide range of Transporters from the camper to emergency vehicles to a contractor's van and much more. Complete construction and technical details and important tips for buying a VW Transporter today round out this wonderful pictorial volume.

Size: 8 1/2 x 11   196 photos   136 pp.
ISBN: 978-0-7643-4074-1   hard cover $29.99

New York City Horsepower: An Oral History of Fast Custom Machines. Michael McCabe. Urban anthropologist Michael McCabe presents the stories behind NYC car and motorcycle builders to reveal an outsider's tale filled with passion, creativity, and high-speed thrills. Based on a year's worth of interviews with nearly 40 legendary custom builders and young builders connecting with the city's hands-on narrative, McCabe offers unique access to their private, creative lives in garages and workshops throughout the five boroughs.

Size: 11 3/4 x 9   796 b/w & color images   304 pp.
ISBN: 978-0-7643-3961-5   hard cover $50.00